YOUR
Career and Life Plan
PORTFOLIO

THIRD EDITION

The Editors @ JIST

JIST Works
America's Career Publisher®

Your Career and Life Plan Portfolio, *Third Edition*

First edition was titled *Creating Your Life's Work Portfolio.*
© 2008 by JIST Publishing

Published by JIST Works, an imprint of JIST Publishing
7321 Shadeland Station, Suite 200
Indianapolis, IN 46256-3923
Phone: 800-648-JIST
E-mail: info@jist.com

Fax: 877-454-7839
Web site: www.jist.com

Note to instructors. Support materials are available for *Your Career and Life Plan Portfolio.* A companion instructor's resources CD-ROM contains helpful guidance and many activities and assignments. Videos on portfolio development, resumes, and job search topics are also available. Call 800-648-JIST for details.

About career materials published by JIST. Our materials encourage people to be self-directed. We work hard to provide excellent content, solid advice, and techniques that get results. If you have questions about this book or other JIST products, call 800-648-JIST or visit www.jist.com.

Quantity discounts are available for JIST products. Have future editions of JIST books automatically delivered to you on publication through our convenient standing order program. Please call 800-648-JIST or visit www.jist.com for a free catalog and more information.

Visit www.jist.com. Find out about our products, get tables of contents and sample pages, order a catalog, and link to other career-related sites. You can also learn more about JIST authors and JIST training available to professionals.

Development Editor: Dave Anderson
Project Editor: Aaron Black
Contributing Writer: Judit E. Price
Copy Editor: Charles Hutchinson
Cover Photo: PhotoAlto/Veer
Cover Designer: Marie Kristine Parial-Leonardo
Interior Designer: Aleata Halbig
Proofreader: Jeanne Clark
Indexer: Cheryl Lenser

Acknowledgment: JIST Publishing editions of this book are a complete revision of an earlier work titled *Life Work Portfolio.* The work was a joint project of the National Occupational Information Coordinating Committee (NOICC), the Maine Occupational Information Coordinating Committee, and the Career Development Training Institute at Oakland University. It was developed with an advisory committee representing job training, adult education, and displaced homemaker programs and was reviewed by a national review team comprising leaders in the career development field. The book was also pilot-tested at major universities, corporate sites, veterans affairs offices, job training programs, and community colleges. While the JIST Publishing editions incorporate major changes, they would not have been possible without the effort of the many people involved in the original *Life Work Portfolio* project.

Printed in the United States of America

13 12 11 10 09 08   9 8 7 6 5 4 3 2 1

ISBN 978-1-59357-435-2

About This
Book

Your portfolio is a collection of records that document your work history and affirm your successes. Your portfolio reflects your career goals and values. It also demonstrates the knowledge and skills you have that will make you an asset to the employer. A portfolio can help both you and an employer understand your career path and the steps you have taken to improve your work life.

In many ways, that is the ultimate goal of this book: to help you identify the steps you need to take to reach your career goals. Along the way, you will create a portfolio to help you get there.

Your Career and Life Plan Portfolio, Third Edition, provides specific information for building your portfolio. But it does much more than show you how to gather and store documents. It explains a step-by-step process for exploring career paths and making decisions. It provides a structure for career planning that you can use more than once as your career develops. It helps you understand what is important to you in your life and work.

In short, this book can coach you through the career exploration, career decision making, and job search process, all the while helping you build a portfolio that will represent your growth as an individual and help you to land the job of your dreams.

Table of Contents

Introduction: Making the Most of Your Career and Life

The purpose of a portfolio is to organize data you will need in your job search. *Your Career and Life Plan Portfolio* goes much further. It provides you with the information you need for creating a portfolio, for making career decisions, and for approaching your life and your job search with confidence. It will help you to understand and articulate the qualities, talents, and accomplishments that make you who you are.

Overview

Your Career and Life Plan Portfolio is organized into three parts.

Part One will introduce you to the role portfolios play in career exploration and the job search. It will show you how to build and organize your portfolio and how to present it to prospective employers. You'll find that Part One

- Defines what a portfolio is and explains why you need one
- Outlines the various types of portfolios
- Provides specific information on creating, organizing, and displaying your portfolio
- Describes the sections of a portfolio and what you might include in each section
- Explains how to use your portfolio in job interviews
- Includes directions for creating an electronic portfolio

Part Two will help you understand who you are and what you have to offer an employer. Part Two of *Your Career and Life Plan Portfolio*

- Describes the effect your career and life values and your learning and personality styles have on your career decisions

- Helps you define your self-management style—how you make decisions, take risks, manage your time, deal with stress, and stay physically and emotionally healthy

- Helps you understand your changing life roles and how they impact your career decisions

- Guides you in describing the experience and skills you have to offer an employer

- Shows how all this can be included and exhibited in your portfolio

Part Three of this book will help you set and achieve your career goals. As you complete the workbook, you will see that Part Three

- Helps you define your ideal job

- Assists you in identifying sources of career information

- Describes the steps involved in making career decisions

- Explains how to evaluate and act on career information

- Guides you in preparing resumes and cover letters

- Provides details about contacting employers, interviewing and following up with employers, and evaluating job offers

- Includes information on being successful and growing in a new job

- Shows how to use your portfolio to help you in each of the preceding steps

Using the Worksheets

This book provides numerous worksheets for you to complete. The worksheets ask you to fill in information, answer questions, or mark checklists. In some cases, you may want to use additional sheets of paper. Also, remember that you can complete the worksheets more than once. You might respond to them as you work through the book now and then again at another stage in your career.

At the end of each section, you'll find a checklist of concepts and skills discussed in that chapter. Mark the items that reflect what you have learned. Then go back through the chapter to learn more about the items you did not check.

Also at the end of most chapters, you will find a checklist of possible items to include in your portfolio. Use this checklist to help you build your portfolio and keep track of your progress.

Remember, this book is designed to help you better understand yourself and to better communicate your positive attributes to employers. Be honest when answering questions and filling in worksheets, and you will soon discover all the great things you have to offer.

Part One

Building Your Portfolio

"Success isn't how far you got, but the distance you traveled from where you started."
—Greek Proverb

"A man's worth is no greater than his ambitions."
—Marcus Aurelius

Chapter 1

Introduction to Portfolios

Welcome to the world of portfolios. The idea of creating a portfolio may be new to you, even though in some ways you have been creating one all your life. We all have dreams, and we all have taken some steps already to fulfill them. A portfolio helps you define those dreams. It also helps you convince others that you have what it takes to pursue them. The information in this chapter will help you answer these questions:

- What is a portfolio?
- How can a portfolio benefit me?
- How do my goals affect my portfolio?
- What kinds of portfolios are there?
- How can I use my portfolio in my job search and beyond?

This book has two purposes. It is designed to help you discover and document everything about yourself that an employer might be interested in. It will also coach you through the process of finding and landing the right job for you. By completing this book, you will have all the information you need to create a portfolio that is representative of your life's work, as well as a plan for building a successful career.

What Is a Portfolio?

A portfolio is a logically organized collection of records that reflects your accomplishments and attributes by highlighting your work and life experience. Your portfolio showcases your success and reflects your career goals and values. It also demonstrates the knowledge, skills, and preferences you have that will make you an asset to an employer. In short, a portfolio tells an employer who you are and what you are capable of.

A portfolio can also help you understand your career path and the steps you have taken to improve your work life. In many ways, that is the aim of this book: to help you identify the steps necessary to reach your career goals.

The use of portfolios is not new. In fact, the term *portfolio* comes from the Italian word *portafoglio,* meaning *to carry leaves or sheets.* The term was used by artists during the Renaissance in reference to the samples of work they showed to potential sponsors. Artists, graphic artists, and teachers have long used portfolios to document their education and experience and showcase their talents. Many high schools and colleges now require students to develop portfolios of their work to help them get a job or further their education.

Portfolios have become extremely powerful tools in today's competitive job market. Advances in technology have made it even easier to store, edit, send, and exhibit examples of our work and records of our accomplishments. Today, people in virtually every profession use portfolios as part of their job search. That said, a well-designed portfolio will still give you an advantage over the majority of job seekers who haven't put in the time and effort to create one of their own.

> Your portfolio showcases your success and reflects your career goals and values. It also demonstrates the knowledge, skills, and preferences you have that will make you an asset to an employer.

Benefits of a Portfolio

Never have our work lives been so uncertain. There was a time when people could expect to get a good job and remain at one company for decades, eventually retiring with a reasonable level of security and a nice watch. In today's global economy, however, the job market is ever-changing. The average worker changes careers 5 times in his or her life and holds an average of 14 jobs. Today's workers must be able to transition into new careers, find new jobs, acquire new skills, and apply existing skills to new uses. In short, workers are more responsible than ever for managing their own careers.

Of course, finding your *first* job, let alone your fourteenth, is hard work. Human resources professionals say that candidates who are prepared, organized, and focused have a definite edge over those who are not. To be successful in your career, you must be *self-directed.* You must take control of your job search, determine your direction, and aggressively advance toward your goal.

> To be successful in your career, you must be self-directed.

You will also need to adopt new tools to help you reach those goals. A portfolio that is professionally organized and presented is a tool you can use to show an employer who you are and the kind of worker you will be. It is also a tool you can use to track your progress during the job search and your success over the course of your career.

When you present yourself to prospective employers, you are faced with the problem of how to present a positive, believable, and accurate picture of yourself. Creating and maintaining a career portfolio will help you do this. Moreover, a portfolio is useful for every kind of job. After all, potential employers are looking for a record of success, regardless of what industry you work in.

Also, creating a portfolio is a wonderful way to build your self-confidence. People tend to minimize their accomplishments and exaggerate their flaws. We can be our own worst critics. A portfolio carefully built over time accentuates the positives and reflects genuine growth and accomplishment. That is why this book doesn't limit itself to the success you might have had in the world of work. Instead, it urges you to explore the range of successes you've had throughout your life.

> Creating a portfolio is a wonderful way to build your self-confidence. A portfolio carefully built over time reflects your genuine growth and accomplishment.

Tip Knowing who you are and what you've accomplished is the key to convincing others of your value.

Many people never take the time to thoroughly study themselves. Yet knowing who you are and what you want in life helps you establish and achieve your goals. You can learn a lot about who you are simply by gathering information for your portfolio.

Responding to Changes in the Workplace

The world of work changes rapidly. Recognizing and anticipating change ensures that you are armed and ready to meet new challenges. Your portfolio reflects the changes in your personal and work lives and provides a framework for managing your career. It can help you cope with change creatively and take away feelings of helplessness.

The personal information in your portfolio reflects the ever-changing balance between your goals, ambition, knowledge, and life experiences. Like a resume, your portfolio includes specific examples of your growth and can be a powerful tool for marketing yourself. The portfolio does not replace the traditional resume but complements it. Think of it as the film for which the resume is merely a preview.

> Your portfolio reflects the changes in your personal and work lives and provides a framework for managing your career.

Assessing Yourself and Your Skills

People who look at portfolios—such as human resources professionals—tend to prize them highly. The reason is that a portfolio is the most objective and thorough assessment of attributes and accomplishments a person can offer. It reflects the opinions of others, giving an employer multiple views of the same subject—*you*. Letters of reference, certificates of achievement, performance evaluations, newspaper or magazine articles reflecting community achievement, thank-you letters from people you have helped, and numerous other documents reflect others' opinions of your accomplishments.

 Portfolios are truly powerful in creating a positive first impression, which is absolutely critical in the initial stages of a job search.

You may know how your experiences and achievements have helped you develop the skills employers seek, but describing how everything fits together is difficult. You must convey your skills and experiences and demonstrate your abilities clearly and objectively. Your portfolio helps you do that.

Demonstrating a Logical Progression

Your portfolio is not just a random file of accomplishments; it is an organized review of your personal and professional growth. The way you organize your portfolio should demonstrate your progress toward achieving one or more measurable goals.

When you show someone your portfolio, you explain what the entries represent and how they fit a pattern of personal and professional growth. This does not mean that your portfolio has to be organized chronologically. For example, your portfolio might start with a section on education and training, then continue with accomplishments and job history, then skills and attributes, then values, and so forth. The point is that any way you decide to organize your portfolio is acceptable as long as it reflects your own personal growth.

> Any way you decide to organize your portfolio is acceptable as long as it reflects your own personal growth.

Portfolios and Goal-Setting

The act of building a portfolio is also an act of self-discovery. Creating a portfolio provides you with an opportunity to consider your future and set goals. This, in turn, helps you to become more self-directed.

When you set goals, you set a destination for yourself that may be difficult to reach, but setting goals can propel you to achieve. Be sure to set specific, attainable, measurable goals. Also consider the scope of your goals: Are they long-range or

> Set specific, attainable, measurable goals and determine a time frame for achieving them.

short-range? What individual steps are required to reach them? Determine a time frame for achieving each goal.

You may also want to set some goals that can never be fully met but that will provide you with lifelong direction. For example, one of your goals might be to keep learning throughout your life. Or you might set a goal of being the best you can be. Short-term objectives that are met along the way can provide you with the strength and courage to continue pursuing your ultimate goals.

My Ultimate Goals

Though you will have an opportunity to identify your specific *career* goals later in this workbook, take the time now to write down two or three *lifelong* goals you would like to work toward.

_____

_____

_____

While *setting* goals is often easy, *achieving* them is not. We all encounter obstacles and opportunities that force us to reevaluate our goals. This is not necessarily bad. Both obstacles and opportunities help us grow and enable us to adapt to the changes of work and life. Those changes are ultimately reflected in your portfolio as well.

The importance of setting goals before you create your portfolio cannot be overstated. Why? Because goal-setting allows you to see the specific actions you need to take. It helps you identify major obstacles, and it forces you to think about ways to deal with them.

Before you can determine your goals and objectives, you must assess your strengths, weaknesses, and values. You also must determine what you want from your career. You need to understand the abilities and skills you have developed through work experience and training. Later chapters will guide you through these steps and show you how all this contributes to your portfolio and your career plan.

Tip Think of your abilities and skills as services you are marketing to potential employers. The portfolio acts as an advertisement for these services.

Types of Portfolios

There are many approaches to creating a portfolio. In general, after you create your basic portfolio and use it in a variety of settings, you will see that it can be fine-tuned to achieve one or more specific objectives. You may find that you need more than one portfolio, with each new portfolio tailored to a specific purpose or career goal.

Bear in mind that most employers are not interested in a long explanation of your life and career. They don't have the time to read an autobiography. However, they *are* interested in anything tangible that helps them decide which candidate to hire. You must choose the examples that best demonstrate your strengths. You must provide information that is clear, relevant, and interesting. Your choice of materials is very important, and that choice reflects the kind of portfolio you create.

> After you create your basic portfolio and use it in a variety of settings, you will see that it can be fine-tuned to achieve one or more specific objectives.

The Master Portfolio

Earlier, we noted that there is no standard way to organize a portfolio; however, you should take into account the criteria of the career you seek. That means you should modify the contents of your portfolio to emphasize the attributes most valued by a specific employer. For example, if a position calls for versatility, you should emphasize your broad training, multiple projects, and diverse accomplishments. If the job calls for a high degree of teamwork, successful examples of working with other people would be best.

For this reason, it is highly recommended that you create a *master portfolio* that contains all the elements discussed in this book. The master portfolio is a complete record of *all* the essentials of your background that you could use in any job search. It includes everything you might show to a potential employer (resumes, recommendations, awards, samples of your work) and some materials that are for your reference only (information on jobs and companies, checklists, a list of contacts, and most of the worksheets from this book). In other words, a master portfolio contains everything you need to manage your career.

The Employment Portfolio

For each situation, you would then create another portfolio from the materials in the master portfolio. This portfolio—called the *employment portfolio* or *job portfolio*—would include information relevant to a specific job search or interview. In other words, it contains the documents, images, and artifacts you think best exhibit your qualifications for the job in question.

As such, your employment portfolio may be different for each job, and certainly for each career, that you pursue. The employment portfolio should be tailored to the specific job you are seeking and showcase the skills, experiences, and attributes that a specific employer would be looking for.

The master portfolio is a tool designed for self-awareness, career exploration, and career and life planning. The employment portfolio is designed to help you get a job. Throughout this book, you will be given suggestions for material to include in both kinds of portfolios. Ultimately, though, what to show to a potential employer is your decision.

Three Portfolio Approaches

While every portfolio is unique to the person and the career goal he or she is seeking, most portfolios take one of these three general approaches:

- **The Experienced Approach:** This type of approach will be particularly useful to you if you have many years of experience and a high level of expertise. It should include numerous examples of your career accomplishments, such as published articles, letters of recommendation, professional awards, technical projects, artwork, or samples. Hiring managers are often interested in knowing what you have accomplished, particularly in technical professions. Therefore, your portfolio should largely reflect your achievements.

- **The Potential Approach:** This approach is useful if you are just entering the job market. Because you have limited work experience, you must convince the interviewer that you are a person with potential. Evidence of your academic achievements, community service, and other accomplishments will impress employers who are more interested in hiring quality individuals than people with an extensive work history. The potential approach emphasizes your personal attributes over your past experience.

- **The Balanced Portfolio:** This portfolio approach works well for people who are targeting a particular job, because this approach blends elements of the other two. Because it includes a little bit of everything, you must be sure not to create an encyclopedia when using this approach.

Tip Regardless of the approach you take, remember to include in your employment portfolio only the examples and information that support your career objective. For example, if you apply for a position as an electronics technician, the fact that you won the Little League Coach-of-the-Year award, while interesting, would not be relevant to your goal. (That information would certainly belong in your *master* portfolio, however, as it is further documentation of your personal growth.)

Portfolios and the Job Search

Because the portfolio tracks your past, present, and future; your goals and your accomplishments; your work history; and your current career objective, it can be useful in all aspects of the job search.

You should use your portfolio as a resource of information about personal attributes, possible contacts, and potential employers. The information it contains can be used to fill out applications, write resumes and cover letters, practice for interviews, and consider job offers. From exploring careers to negotiating salary, you can use the documents contained in the portfolio to help guide your decisions.

> From exploring careers to negotiating salary, the documents contained in the portfolio should help guide and inform your decisions.

Most importantly, your portfolio should grow with you. You will continue to build your portfolio long after you've accepted a job offer. Because of the ever-changing nature of today's workplace, it is important to keep your portfolio up-to-date. If done well, a master portfolio will be there to see you through your entire career, evolving from one experience to the next.

Portfolios and Job Interviews

While a portfolio serves many functions and can be useful throughout your working life, it still has one primary function: to help you get the job you want by showing why you are the right person for it. Interviews usually provide the best chance to make that connection.

After you have collected the material that will be included in your employment portfolio, you are ready to think about how you will present the information to employers. Remember that, to the untrained eye, one portfolio entry carries as much weight as any other. A quick review of the contents does not tell interviewers what you can do for their organization. In fact, the parts of your portfolio that relate to the position you are applying for may be spread across several documents. Therefore, it is your responsibility to make the specific connections between the job you are applying for and the contents of your portfolio. Following are some suggestions for how.

> It is your responsibility to make the specific connections between the job you are applying for and the contents of your portfolio.

Before the Interview

You must be able to talk about your portfolio examples as you show them to an employer. This requires some preparation.

Identify items in your portfolio that show you have skills and achievements directly related to the job you want. Think about how you could describe each skill or achievement to an employer. Think of these descriptions as short stories. Practice saying them aloud. No description should last more than 2 minutes. In each story, describe your skills, the actual problem or need you faced, the action you took to solve the problem or meet the need, and the results. Remember that you want to convince the employer that you can do the job.

> You must be able to talk about your portfolio examples as you show them to an employer. Being modest at an interview is not a virtue.

As you decide which portfolio examples to present to an employer, consider all your accomplishments—even those you did not have to work hard to achieve. An interviewer might be impressed by an accomplishment that does not seem important to you. Being modest at an interview is not a virtue.

During the Interview

When you present your portfolio to an employer, focus on information that relates directly to the job you want. Employers want to know that you can apply your skills and achievements to *their* organization's problems and needs. Use your portfolio examples to reinforce your descriptions of your achievements. You gain credibility with the employer when you are able to both describe and show examples of what you have done.

And remember, not everything you might put into your master portfolio is intended to be shown to every employer. Be selective. Pick and choose the examples that best prove you have the skills, values, and experience needed for the job.

> You gain credibility with the employer when you are able to both describe and show examples of what you have done.

▶ Let's Review

Complete the following checklist. Review information in this chapter that applies to any items you are unable to check.

End of Chapter Checklist

❑ I know what a portfolio is and how it can benefit me.

❑ I know how my goals affect my portfolio.

❑ I know the difference between a master portfolio and an employment portfolio. I also know three basic approaches to building my portfolio.

❑ I know how a portfolio can assist me in my job search.

❑ I know how to use my portfolio in a job interview.

Date: _____

Chapter 2

Portfolio Design

Before you define your goals and gather your materials, it helps to visualize what your portfolio will look like. This chapter will help you answer these questions:

- What information should be included in my portfolio?
- How should my portfolio be organized?
- Do I need an electronic portfolio?
- How do I store and present an electronic portfolio?
- What are some things I should or should not do when preparing an electronic portfolio?
- How can I use my portfolio to market myself?

Remember that the portfolio you ultimately end up showing an employer should be geared to the job you are interested in. This means that both the contents of your portfolio and the way it looks may change to match the situation. Keep this point in mind as you decide what to include and what format to use.

The Process

The development of your portfolio is a multistep process. It requires self-reflection, honest self-assessment, and just plain hard work. Presenting all your experience, achievements, and goals through a collection of documents is a challenge.

You can think of your portfolio as a marketing tool designed to sell *you*—your skills, experience, and attributes—to a potential employer. To do this, you must evaluate yourself objectively, understand your strengths and weaknesses, and develop a set of meaningful goals. You must also seek out potential employers whose needs fit your skills. The chapters that follow will help you with each of these tasks.

 Remember, a portfolio is a living document. It must be updated, reshaped, and modified as you travel along your career path. The more experience you gain, the more employers will expect from you. You must show them that you can meet their expectations.

Creating your portfolio can be a rewarding experience. It requires you to take a close look at where you have been, where you are now, and where you want to be. It can empower you to become more self-directed and take control of your career.

Getting Started

Start developing your portfolio by taking a personal inventory. Review your skills, your accomplishments, and your personal and professional goals and priorities. Follow these steps:

1. **Define yourself.** List your credentials, interests, skills, strengths, and weaknesses.

2. **Define your opportunities.** List the knowledge and skills you have that are most needed by employers, the kinds of work you would enjoy doing, and the types of organizations that appeal to you.

3. **Define a strategy.** Focus on a certain job or career.

4. **Define your approach.** Determine how you will present yourself and what you will do to make a good first impression.

As you collect items to include in your portfolio, a pattern will begin to emerge. Your goals will become clearer, and you will discover new strategies for marketing yourself to an employer. When you are finished creating your portfolio (and with this book), you will have the foundation for your career plan.

Tip Many occupations and industries are represented by organizations that set standards for their members. These organizations describe what people in a certain occupation should be able to do and how they should conduct their business. Join organizations for people in your profession. This will help you understand what will be expected from you. In your portfolio, include information about your membership in these organizations as well.

Choosing and Organizing Content

Though every portfolio is as unique as the person who creates it, most portfolios share the same kinds of information. In general, this is the information that most employers are interested in as well. As you build your portfolio, carefully consider these seven categories:

- Personal Information
- Personal Goals and History

- Values

- Accomplishments and Job History

- Skills and Attributes

- Education and Training

- Testimonials and Recommendations

If you are new to portfolios, consider making each of these categories a separate section of your master portfolio. As you create your first portfolio, you may find that you have more materials than you need. Gathering as much information as possible allows you the flexibility of choosing the best examples. Individual bits and pieces of information may not say much about you, but a bigger picture develops when you put the pieces together.

> Individual bits and pieces of information may not say much about you, but a bigger picture develops when you put the pieces together.

Also, consider making a separate section in your master portfolio where you can file the checklists and worksheets from this workbook as well as other reference material. Storing these items in your portfolio makes the information they contain readily available. Just remember that the materials in this extra section will be for your reference only. Be sure to remove them when creating an employment portfolio to show to an employer.

Let's look at the various sections of your portfolio in more detail.

Personal Information

Locating and gathering personal information may be the most time-consuming aspect of creating your portfolio. However, it is also the most critical. You will be asked to provide this information every time you fill out a job application or interview for a job.

> Locating and gathering personal information may be the most time-consuming aspect of creating your portfolio. However, it is also the most critical.

You may think that your personal information is just statistical data, but it can actually help you see yourself as other people see you. Having a good sense of self helps you in all aspects of your life's work. In this section of your portfolio, include copies of your

- Birth certificate

- Health records

- Picture identification or current photo

- Social Security card

- Passport

- Driver's license

- Work permit

- Noncitizen status papers

- Survey, test, or assessment results

Including copies of these documents in your portfolio ensures that you will have this information when you need it. To keep your original documents safe and in good condition, make photocopies of the originals and place the copies in your portfolio.

In addition to the items in the preceding list, consider including the following worksheet in your portfolio. Employment laws vary from state to state, so you may not be asked to provide all the information listed on the worksheet. However, you should be prepared to provide the information if asked.

My Personal Information

Full name _____

Other names I have used _____

Street address _____

City _____ State/Province _____ ZIP _____

Previous address _____

City _____ State/Province _____ ZIP _____

Telephone numbers: Home _____ Work _____

Pager _____ Cell phone _____

E-mail address _____

Mailing address (if different from above) _____

City _____ State/Province _____ ZIP _____

Social Security number _____

Driver's license number _____

Date of birth _____ Place of birth _____

U.S. citizen? (Y/N) _____ If not, current status _____

Visa Registration number _____

Other: _____

_____

_____

Personal Goals and History

Generally placed at the beginning of a portfolio, Personal Goals and History is a short section describing your career goals and objectives. It is a good place to comment on your career progression as well. Such a section might include a detailed action plan, a timeline for your past and future accomplishments, or a personal mission statement. Educators, for example, might include a statement about their teaching philosophies here.

As you review the other sections of your portfolio with an interviewer, point out the connections between those sections and the Personal Goals and History section. This shows how your experiences have helped you attain your goals. It also is an excellent way to emphasize your commitment to a career direction. Chapter 3 will help you document your personal goals and history.

My Personal Goals and History

Think about your career goals and objectives and write a statement briefly describing them here: _____

_____

_____

Values

Your values are the basis of your motivation, interests, desires, and attitudes. Your values define what you want from life and from your career. Clarifying your values will give you a sense of direction and purpose, especially when making career decisions.

The Values section of a portfolio is the most difficult to define and document. However, employers want to ensure that new hires conform to their organizations' values. Businesses often have their own corporate values statements, meant to encourage a cooperative work environment based on trust and open-mindedness. These statements are designed to foster an atmosphere free of harassment and discrimination. They encourage a commitment to quality and integrity in the company's dealings with employees, vendors, and customers. Thus, any examples in your work experience that reflect such values should be included.

> Clarifying your values will give you a sense of direction and purpose, especially when making career decisions.

Tip As an employee, you will be the most content and productive in jobs that allow you to satisfy your own important values. Therefore, you should always consider your values when exploring career options.

For this section you might include documentation of your public and community service, your leadership, your church involvement, or your participation in charitable organizations. Such involvement shows your values in action. Chapter 3 will help you to articulate your values.

My Values

Think about one document or statement you would like to include in the Values section of your portfolio and write it here: _____

_____

_____

Accomplishments and Job History

Even though each section of your portfolio is important, your Accomplishments and Job History section will probably be the most interesting to employers. For starters, this is a good place for your resume (more information on resumes can be found in Chapter 6). This section should also describe job-related accomplishments clearly and include both paid and unpaid work experience. Relevant information for each job includes a complete job description, the organization's address, your supervisor's name, and any performance evaluations. References and letters of recommendation are extremely helpful, though they often comprise their own section.

Tip One document may serve multiple purposes. For example, a Master Automotive Technician Certification showcases both experience and skills.

Finally, visuals are extremely valuable. One picture can be worth a thousand words; therefore, feel free to add artwork, photos, graphs, designs, articles, or any other visual aids that reinforce your message. Examples might include pictures and descriptions of products you designed or sold, marketing pieces, profitability charts, customer comment cards, or even news stories written about you or your work. These artifacts provide evidence of your accomplishments and can be referred to throughout an interview. Later chapters will help you record your accomplishments and job history.

My Accomplishments and Job History

Think about one document or example you would like to include in the Accomplishments and Job History section of your portfolio and note it here: _____

_____

_____

Skills and Attributes

Employers are looking for workers with the right skills for the job. Any skill that relates to a specific position should be clearly identified in your portfolio. These skills may be acquired through formal or informal training or on the job. Any documentation that shows your skills in use will be helpful as well.

Special knowledge that is unique to a profession can also be considered a skill. For example, you may have an understanding of financial documents, contracts, healthcare regulations, or market research. This knowledge contributes to your overall skill set, so be sure to include it in your portfolio. In many cases, what you know can be even more important than what you have done. Feel free to include any special skills or knowledge acquired from hobbies or leisure activities as well.

> Special knowledge that is unique to a profession can also be considered a skill. In many cases, what you know can be even more important than what you have done.

Attributes are intangible qualities and may be difficult to quantify, but they are highly regarded by employers. The abilities to communicate effectively, to work in a team setting, to learn quickly, to follow instructions, to accept criticism gracefully, and to be creative are all examples of positive attributes. Any documents or information you have that demonstrate these attributes should be part of your portfolio. Chapter 4 will help you define your best skills and attributes.

My Skills and Attributes

Think about one document or example you would like to include in the Skills and Attributes section of your portfolio and note it here: _____

_____

_____

Education and Training

The Education and Training section should include a complete education and training record. Course descriptions, transcripts, and examples of completed projects can be very helpful. Documents of achievement from seminars, workshops, and professional development courses can also be included.

If you are just entering the workforce or have limited experience, invest careful thought and planning in this section. Your academic achievements may have to substitute for a lack of work experience. On the flipside, if you have significant work experience, you will not have to spend as much time on this section. However, your most impressive academic achievements should still be included.

 Lifelong learning has become particularly important in today's world of work. This refers to the efforts you make to continue learning and gaining new skills even after you have finished your formal schooling. Be sure to include any evidence of your commitment to lifelong learning in your portfolio.

Also consider any experiential learning. This is learning you gain through life experiences, and it cannot be easily categorized. Later chapters will help you document your education and training experience and even explore future educational opportunities.

My Education and Training

Think about one document or example you would like to include in the Education and Training section of your portfolio and note it here: _____

_____

_____

Evaluations and Recommendations

Any form of positive feedback should be included in your portfolio. A good evaluation is one that is specific. In an interview, you should show how the skills and attributes described in your evaluations relate to the achievements included in other sections of your portfolio. Your portfolio will be more credible if you can show how your skills and abilities are demonstrated over and over in your performance.

> Your portfolio will be more credible if you can show how your skills and abilities are demonstrated over and over in your performance.

Awards and certificates that demonstrate achievement in other fields should also be included in this section of your portfolio. Examples include honors from membership in organizations or through volunteer and community involvement. These honors show your professionalism, cooperation, and team spirit.

Finally, if you have any letters of recommendation, consider making them a part of your portfolio as well. Such letters act as an instant personal reference and give future employers the chance to see what past employers liked best about you.

My Evaluations and Recommendations

Think about one document or example you would like to include in the Evaluations and Recommendations section of your portfolio and note it here: _____

_____

_____

Building the Portfolio

Once you have gathered all your materials, you are ready to build your portfolio. You can arrange the various sections in any order, but remember that the goal is to use the portfolio to get a job. You should begin with a simple table of contents that identifies the sections of the portfolio. A suggested flow for your portfolio is

1. Personal Goals and History

2. Values

3. Accomplishments and Job History

4. Skills and Attributes

5. Education and Training

6. Evaluations and Recommendations

7. Reference Materials (including personal documentation and other resources not intended to be shown to an employer)

The order suggested here is appropriate for the typical job seeker. Remember that content and presentation are far more important than the order of the sections in your portfolio. Also keep in mind that you may choose to emphasize some sections and materials over others depending on the job you are seeking.

Tip The Values section and the Personal Goals and History section should be short unless you have something especially significant to say. The more work experience you have, the more emphasis you should give to the Accomplishments and Job History section.

Measuring the Results

Reviewing your portfolio is a good way to see if the contents are properly focused. It also gives you an opportunity to think about whether your planned career path is really right for you. If you *are* content with your career goals, focus on the portfolio as a vehicle for achieving them.

Before using your portfolio in job interviews, review it to be sure it says what you want it to say. Then ask other people to look at your portfolio and tell you whether they think the goals you set are truly reflected in the portfolio. After a job interview, think about whether the portfolio items you used were effective.

Displaying Your Portfolio

The following information refers only to paper-based portfolios. The key point regarding presentation can be summed up in one word: professionalism. No matter how impressive or exciting the content of your portfolio may be, it may not produce the desired results if it does not have a professional look and feel.

Original documents, excluding IDs, should be included when practical, with each item enclosed in its own transparent plastic cover or sheet protector. You may be concerned about maintaining certain original documents in good condition (such as a transcript or diploma). If so, you can include clean, clear copies instead.

Use separators and typed labels to divide each section of your portfolio. You can use a large artist-type cover, but most people use a nice three-ring binder. Include a cover sheet on the front of the binder, noting that this is a portfolio and giving your name, address, e-mail address, and telephone number. Be sure the size of the binder is consistent with the volume of material. The binder should not look empty, but it should also not look stuffed.

Graphs, pictures, drawings, blueprints, designs, and any other visual aids should look appealing and be in color, if possible. Handle the portfolio carefully. Remove any smudges or handprints. Keep it away from puppies, small children, and cups of coffee. After you make it presentable, you'll want to keep it that way.

> **Tip** Appearance can make a difference. Your ability to present your material professionally can give you an edge in the job search.

Electronic Portfolios

Much of the job search process is already handled electronically. Resumes and cover letters are formatted for electronic submission, and many job applicants have professional Web sites listing their accomplishments. For job seekers who take the time to create a portfolio in the first place, the question of whether to go electronic is fast becoming a "no-brainer." This is especially true for people in creative professions (such as artists or Web designers). It is also true for those working in any business that uses technology in the normal course of its work (which is most of us).

A Cautionary Note

Electronic media are all the rage. People commonly put their portfolios on CDs, DVDs, or flash drives, or send the documents by e-mail. Personal Web sites and blogs are everywhere. The natural assumption is that these media will soon overtake hard-copy versions of the portfolio, but that assumption is incorrect. Recruiters and human resources personnel do not have time to consider all the information you could include on a CD or Web site. They do not even have time to look at all the resumes they receive.

No matter how well organized your electronic portfolio is, an employer may view it simply as a set of random documents. However, when you present your hard-copy portfolio in an interview, you can put each item in context. Each entry emphasizes the points you wish to communicate. Interviews are intensely human encounters, where the parties have an opportunity to meet face to face and size each other up. In this context, a hard-copy version of your portfolio is most effective.

The Role of Electronic Portfolios

Even though you should not abandon your hard-copy portfolio, you should consider developing an electronic version as well. Electronic portfolios are a relatively inexpensive way to market yourself. You can use your portfolio to reach a lot of people in a short time, allowing you to distribute information about yourself to employers who would not otherwise know about you.

Although employers will spend little time viewing your CD or Web site, an electronic portfolio can still make a positive impression. Web-based portfolios are still uncommon, so recruiters or human resources specialists might look at your portfolio carefully if it catches their eyes. This won't get you a job, but it might get you an interview.

> You can use your electronic portfolio to reach a lot of people in a short time, allowing you to distribute information about yourself to employers who would not otherwise know about you.

Tip A Web-based portfolio can be a convenient way to update your current job accomplishments as you prepare for the next job, promotion, or raise. It also makes long-distance networking easier.

Generally, the philosophy and contents of an electronic portfolio mirror those of the paper version. However, keep in mind that you can select the material you will show in an interview, but you cannot select what material an employer will choose to view or not view on your Web site or CD. For this reason, you must be particularly careful about what you include.

The electronic portfolio can be an exciting tool to help in the job search. The more technically proficient you are, the more opportunity you have to be creative. For example, simple text documents can be enhanced in marvelous ways through software programs such as Microsoft PowerPoint. Graphics software, such as Adobe Photoshop, can add color, design, emphasis, and special effects.

To create an electronic portfolio, you must be able to use the available tools. This requires some basic computer and software skills. The good news is that even a beginner can learn to create electronic documents fairly quickly.

Creating a CD

A portfolio on a CD can be easily mailed or given to employers. The cost of copying (burning) files to CDs has decreased dramatically, which means that mailing CDs to potential employers has become an effective way to introduce yourself and showcase your strengths. By using rewritable CDs, you can even update the documents in the portfolio as necessary. Just be certain to have spare copies in reserve and to keep all the electronic files on your computer for easy access.

> **Tip** Consider putting your digital portfolio on a USB flash drive. Unlike a paper-based portfolio or even a CD, these devices fit easily in your pocket and can be carried with you everywhere you go. This way, you will always have your portfolio with you to show to potential employers . . . provided they have a computer. But these days, what employer doesn't?

Creating a Web Site

Unlike a portfolio on CD, a Web site can and should be modified often. By putting your portfolio on the Web, you make it instantly available to millions of potential employers (and hundreds of millions of other people as well). Designing a Web site is not difficult or expensive, but it does require some artistic flair. Inexpensive, easy-to-use software is available to help you achieve a professional look.

To create your own Web-based portfolio, you need three things:

1. **You need Web-creation software.** Software for beginners is available for as little as $20. This software will walk you through the process of building a Web site, tell you how to register with a Web hosting service (usually their own), and get you started online. If you are artistic, you can create an impressive Web site with low-cost software. Most Web hosting services (such as Yahoo!'s Geocities) will provide free software for creating your own site.

2. **You need a domain name or Uniform Resource Locator (URL).** Technically, the terms *domain name* and *URL* have different definitions, but they are often used interchangeably. Your domain name is your Web address. For information about registering a domain name, simply do an Internet search for the keywords *Domain Name,* and you will find sources and instructions for registering.

    You might choose a name such as www.billsportfolio.com or www.hiresuzy.org. You can make up any name or combination of names, check online for availability, and register the name with one of the online domain name services. Current costs are about $5–$15 per year.

3. **You need a Web hosting service.** This is the organization that will host your Web site on its server, create an e-mail account for you, and provide a range of other services. Prices vary depending on the kinds of services you want. You can easily find information about these services by searching the Web with the keywords *Web Hosting Services*. Most Web hosting services will provide the things discussed in the first two items as well.

In addition, numerous Web sites are available to help you create your online portfolio. The following list is by no means complete, but it does represent a cross section of the available information. For more resources on creating electronic portfolios, see the appendix.

www.albion.edu/digitalportfolio

www.electronicportfolios.com

www.quintcareers.com/career_portfolios.html

www.bsu.edu/students/careers/documents/portfoli/

www.portronics.com

www.regent.edu/acad/schcou/portfolios/index.htm

www.efoliominnesota.com

http://depts.washington.edu/geogjobs/Careers/pfolresources.html

www.ub-careers.buffalo.edu/portfolios.shtml

http://cas.humber.ca/ecp.htm

Dos and Don'ts of Web-Based Portfolios

- **Do** carefully choose the information you put on the Web site. You will not have much opportunity for explanations. Consequently, the Web content must be selective and professionally presented.

- **Do** update your Web site frequently. You can buy inexpensive software that lets you do virtually anything. Your hosting service can also help.

- **Do** include some visual appeal. Don't go overboard with space-eating graphics or animations, but be sure your Web site has a professional look and feel.

- **Do** include information about how employers can contact you by telephone, fax, and e-mail.

- **Do** take a look at other Web sites and ask your friends and colleagues for suggestions.

- **Do** print out color copies of your Web site for interviews if you don't use a hard-copy portfolio.

- **Don't** indicate on your Web site that you are looking for work. You don't want your current employer to suspect the reason behind your electronic portfolio.

- **Don't** spam. The term *spam* refers to unsolicited e-mail. Target your electronic portfolio to a carefully chosen audience that matches your career goals.

- **Don't** have advertisements on your Web site. Pay for a hosting service that is advertisement free.

- **Don't** put your picture on your Web site. You want to avoid any issues relative to employment laws.

- **Don't** include too much personal information. Be cautious. Remember that anyone can view your online portfolio.

Portfolios and Personal Branding

Today's job market requires workers to be marketers; we must be able to sell an employer on our credentials and potential. In short, in everything we do, we create an image of ourselves for others to see. That image becomes our personal brand.

Your portfolio can go a long way toward establishing your personal brand. While its individual components vary, the sum of those parts creates a complete image. That image should be positive, energetic, professional, and confident. But it should also be uniquely you. Be sure that your portfolio design matches your personality and emphasizes those characteristics that set you apart from the crowd—that make you a unique brand name that employers will be interested in.

> Be sure that your portfolio design matches your personality and emphasizes those characteristics that set you apart from the crowd—that make you a unique brand name that employers will be interested in.

The remaining chapters of this book will walk you more specifically through the creation of your portfolio. Along the way, you will set your career goals, define your skills, document your experiences, and devise a plan to help you find and get the job you want.

Remember that the creation of your portfolio is about much more than collecting a set of documents to show an employer. It is about defining who you are and what you want to accomplish, creating a plan for your career and for your life.

Career and Life Plan Portfolio Checklist

Consider adding the following artifacts, documents, and resources to your portfolio:

❏ Personal information, such as a birth certificate, passport, driver's license, and assessment results

❏ Information concerning your values, including a personal values statement and records of public and community service

❏ Documents describing your career goals, such as an action plan or mission statement

❏ Documents detailing your accomplishments and work history, such as evaluations, awards, and samples of your work

❏ Documents that exhibit your skills and attributes

❏ Documents that show your achievements in education and training, including transcripts and examples of your work

❏ Positive evaluations and letters of recommendation

▶ Let's Review

Complete the following checklist. Review information in this chapter that applies to any items you are unable to check.

End of Chapter Checklist

❏ I know how to choose and evaluate documents to be included in my portfolio.

❏ I know of one or more people I can ask to review my portfolio.

❏ I have thought about what items to include in the Personal Information section of my portfolio.

❏ I know one item I want to include in the Personal Goals and History section.

❏ I know one thing I want to include in the Values section.

❏ I have thought about what items I want to include in the Accomplishments and Job History section.

❏ I can describe one item I could include in the Skills and Attributes section.

❏ I have thought of one item I want to include in the Education and Training section.

❏ I know one item to include in the Testimonials and Recommendations section of my portfolio.

❏ I can describe what an electronic portfolio is.

❏ I am considering creating a portfolio CD.

❏ I understand the basics of creating a Web site.

❏ I know where to find online support for creating my Web site.

❏ I can name some of the dos and don'ts of creating a Web-based portfolio.

Date: _____

Part Two

Understanding Yourself

"I wonder if I've been changed in the night? Let me think: was I the same when I got up this morning? I almost think I can remember feeling a little different. But if I'm not the same, the next question is, 'Who in the world am I?' Ah, that's the great puzzle!"

—Lewis Carroll, *Alice's Adventures in Wonderland*

Chapter 3

Who You Are

Now that you have a general understanding of what a portfolio is and what it looks like, it's time to put yours together. To build, organize, and use your portfolio, you need to first understand who you are. You have interests, abilities, and values that make you unique. Gathering information about yourself is the first step on the road to a satisfying occupation. This chapter will help you answer these questions:

- What do I value in my life and career?

- What are my learning and personality styles?

- What self-management skills do I need for making decisions, taking risks, managing my time, dealing with stress, staying healthy, and finding emotional support?

- What are my past, current, and future roles in life, and how do they affect my career decisions?

- What kind of work am I most interested in doing?

Knowing the answers to these questions can help you cope with job change, choose a new career direction, and persuade employers to hire you.

In addition to helping you find an ideal career match, the self-knowledge you gain from working through this chapter can also help you set personal goals and can improve your interviewing skills. After all, the more you know about yourself, the easier it is to convince others of your values, skills, and attributes.

Most of what is discussed in this chapter will not be included directly in the portfolio you show to employers. However, everything that is discussed can help you make the right choices as you explore career options and prepare for your job search.

Values

Who you are is a reflection of what you value. Each of us has our own ideas about what's important, and those values motivate us, both in work and in life. If you can balance what's important in your life with what's important in your work, you will find satisfaction both on and off the job.

You may not find many career options that match *all* your career and life values. However, for an occupation to be satisfying, it should fulfill many of your important values. As you explore various career options, match what you have learned about your values to the descriptions of the occupations. After you talk to an employer and interview for a job, you can better compare your list of values to what the job has to offer.

> As you explore various career options, match what you have learned about your values to the descriptions of the occupations.

Career Values

If you value the work you do, you are more committed to working and doing the job well. Here are a few examples of work values:

- Income
- Safety
- Work environment
- Skills development
- Acknowledgment and appreciation
- Teamwork
- Change and variety
- Independence
- Creativity
- Competition
- Advancement
- Structure and security
- Helping others
- Taking risks

> If you value the work you do, you are more committed to working and doing the job well.

If you have difficulty identifying what you value, talk with close friends or family members. They may be able to give you some insight.

Tip Self-assessment instruments can also help you discover more about your values. Several types of self-scoring instruments may be available at your nearby high school, adult education center, college, or university. Most are available for free or a small fee.

The following worksheet will help you think about what your career values are. Place check marks in one of the three columns to show how significant each career value is to you.

My Career Values

	Essential	Significant	Insignificant
Accomplishment			
Authority			
Belonging			
Challenge			
Competition			
Contribution			
Creativity			
Flexibility			
Income			
Independence			
Influence			
Order			
Peace of mind			
Power			
Prestige			
Recognition			
Responsibility			
Security			
Service to others			
Structure			
Variety			

Life Values

You've thought about what is important to you in your career. Now think about those things that are important to you outside work. Here are a few examples of life values:

- Leisure time
- Family
- Hobbies or sports
- Friendships
- Community activities
- Religious activities

It is important to find a career that doesn't conflict with your life values and maybe even complements them. If family is most important, you should look for careers that provide flexible schedules or enough time off to spend at home. If personal hobbies are most important to you, consider career fields that will let you use the same skills those hobbies require.

On the following worksheet, create a list of your 10 most important life values. Then number the values in order of their importance to you. Share the list with people who know you well. Ask them if it matches what they know about you. Consider their input, but be sure your list reflects what *you* think is important, not what *others* say should be important.

> Be sure your list of life values reflects what *you* think is important, not what *others* say should be important.

My Life Values

Here's a list of the 10 life values that are most important to me, ranked in order of importance.

_____   _____

_____   _____

_____   _____

_____   _____

_____   _____

_____   _____

_____   _____

_____   _____

_____   _____

_____   _____

Learning Styles

In Chapter 4 of this book, you will have an opportunity to think about the skills you are interested in learning and those you can offer an employer. To learn new skills more easily, you should first determine your personal learning style. Personal learning style simply means *the way you learn best.*

Most people believe that learning and education are the same and that they come primarily, if not exclusively, from going to school. But that's simply not true. Take a look at the difference between education and learning in your own life. You are a student for several years, but you are a learner for a lifetime.

> People learn in different ways, so understanding your personal learning style is vitally important.

People learn in different ways, so understanding your personal learning style is vitally important. The two basic types of learning are traditional learning and experiential learning:

1. Some of us learn best by reading books, listening to lectures, and participating in activities led by a teacher or instructor. This type of learning is called **traditional learning.** It is also sometimes referred to as *classroom learning.*

2. Others of us prefer to learn by doing something, by practicing, or by experimenting on our own. This is called **experiential learning.**

For most of us, the transition from student to self-directed learner is difficult. We must work to develop a learning style that is appropriately balanced between traditional and experiential learning. You should find the right combination of learning styles for you. If you know what kind of learner you are, and if you assume active responsibility for your learning, you will greatly increase your chances for career success.

 Tip You could start discovering your learning style by using a self-scoring inventory such as the Kolb Learning Style Inventory (LSI). Feel free to include in your portfolio the results of any tests or assessments you take.

Employers often express reservations about people who are strongly traditional or strongly experiential learners. They complain that purely traditional learners know a lot about theory but are often ineffective at applying that theory in the real world. They complain that purely experiential learners may be able to do something in one particular situation but are often not able to perform in unfamiliar settings. Also, because they don't understand the theory behind what they are doing, experiential learners are often unable to tell other people how to do it.

After you know what kind of learner you are, you may want to make some adjustments for balance. For example, if you find that you are very much a traditional learner, you may want to consider trying to learn something by just doing it instead of by reading a book or watching a video.

You must work to define your style and then find a career that allows you to learn new skills in ways you are comfortable with.

You must work to define your style, strike the right balance between traditional and experiential learning, and find a career that allows you to learn new skills in ways you are comfortable with. In addition, you should provide proof to potential employers of your ability to learn quickly through whichever style fits you best. Such proof should be included in your portfolio.

Personality Styles

Just as understanding your learning style can help you develop new skills, knowing your personality style can help you find a job that fits you. Essentially, your personality style is the combination of your attitudes, feelings, and desires that dictate your patterns of behavior. In other words, your personality style is the sum of those personal traits that cause you to act as you do.

Tip Numerous personality tests and assessments are available to help you discover your style. Be sure to choose an assessment that provides information related to career choices, such as the *SDS*, *MBTI*, or *CEI*. For more information on assessments and other resources, see the appendix. Consider including in your portfolio the results of any assessments you take.

The following chart gives some examples of how your personality impacts your selection of a career.

If you like...	Do not select an occupation in which...
Change and variety in your work	You do the same tasks day after day
Meeting and talking with new people	You work alone in an office
Planning your own activities	You have to follow a set schedule

Obviously, you want to find a career that is a good fit for your personality. Employers also want to find workers whose personality styles fit well with their organizations. Being able to articulate your personality style in interviews and show how it matches up well with jobs you are interested in can increase your chance of career success.

As you mature and grow, your personality naturally changes. When you review your personality style, you may discover areas you would like to develop more fully. Use the following worksheet to begin thinking about your personality style. This information can also be helpful as you search for careers or prepare for an interview.

Employers want to find workers whose personality styles fit well with their organizations.

My Personality Style

Two ways to describe my behavior at work are

1. _____

2. _____

Two ways to describe my behavior at home are

1. _____

2. _____

Two ways I react to work situations are

1. _____

2. _____

Two ways I react to life situations are

1. _____

2. _____

I would describe my personality as

_____

_____

People who have known me for a long time would describe my personality as

_____

_____

People who have met me only once would describe my personality as

_____

_____

Self-Management Styles

Self-management style is a term used to describe the way you handle life—particularly its challenges, choices, and conflicts. It refers to the following:

- Making decisions
- Taking risks
- Managing your time
- Dealing with stress
- Staying emotionally and physically healthy

These aspects of your self-management style are interrelated. Understanding your self-management style is important when you are choosing a career direction, making a career transition, or interviewing with a prospective employer. Employers are especially interested in how you deal with stress, how you manage your time and resources, and how you make decisions.

Tip If your current self-management strategies aren't working, think about trying some new ones. Talk with people you admire and ask them about their self-management styles. Visit your local library or bookstore to find resources to help you.

The worksheets on the following pages will help you determine if your self-management style is working for you. If you aren't entirely satisfied with how you handle circumstances and events in your life, you're not alone. The good news is that self-management skills can be learned and improved.

Tip Managing your personal life makes it easier to manage your career. You need a self-management style that helps you achieve good results in all areas of your life.

Remember, successfully managing your personal life makes it easier to manage your career. You need a self-management style that helps you achieve good results in all areas of your life.

Making Decisions

How do you usually make decisions? This is one aspect of your self-management style that is of particular interest to an employer. Here are some guidelines for effective decision making:

1. **Define the problem.** State the underlying problem, not the surface problem. Be specific. State the problem as a question.

2. **State the goal.** Clearly describe the outcomes you want.

3. **List alternative solutions.** Determine which are safe and which require risk. List the possible outcomes of each solution.

4. **Collect information.** Expand your list of alternatives. Describe the kind of information you need and where you can obtain it. Decide whether the information is relevant to the problem.

5. **Compare.** Compare several alternatives with what you know about your values, your commitments to other people, your resources, and your constraints.

6. **Decide.** Choose one alternative that is consistent with your stated goal.

7. **Take action on your choice.** Determine how you will implement your choice. Decide what actions you can take now and later.

8. **Review your choice periodically.** Make sure that the effects of your actions are helping you reach your stated goal.

9. **Make new decisions as your situation changes.** If something comes along to derail your plan, go back to step one and reevaluate.

Following these guidelines when you are considering career and life changes can help you make decisions. Going through such a methodical process ensures that you've thought through the decision. Later chapters will take you through this process with regards to your career.

Taking Risks

All decisions involve some level of risk, and your risk-taking style influences your decisions. Here are five approaches to taking risks:

- **The Wish Approach:** The most important thing is to reach the desired outcome. Ignores risks.

- **The Safe Approach:** The most important thing is not to fail. Chooses the outcome with the highest probability of success.

- **The Escape Approach:** Chooses no outcome. Lets fate dictate.

- **The High-Risk Approach:** The most important thing is to take a risk. Chooses the outcome that is most likely to fail but may yield a very desirable outcome.

- **The Combination Approach:** Risks and outcomes are both important. Balances a highly desirable outcome with a calculated risk.

For some people, changing occupations, getting more education, or looking for work may be exciting. For others, these activities may feel risky and cause anxiety. As you think about your risk-taking style, consider the following:

- How much risk can I handle right now? How much risk do I want to handle in my career? In my next job?

- Do some things seem risky just because I don't know much about them?

- Do I know someone who has been faced with this kind of risk? Can I talk to that person?

- How will I benefit from change? Is the benefit worth the risk? What will happen if I don't take this chance?

- What can I do to make the change less risky?

- Who can give me support and encourage me?

> **Tip** Knowing your risk-taking style can be important for employers as well. Some jobs almost require workers to take risks (such as day-trader on the stock market), whereas other jobs highly discourage it (such as nuclear power plant operator). Research the job to see whether it matches your own acceptable level of risk.

Part Two: Understanding Yourself

The following worksheet can help you understand your risk-taking style more clearly. This, in turn, can help you set your immediate career objectives and long-term goals.

My Risk-Taking Style

I remember times in my life when I was faced with several changes at once or with one life-changing decision.

I was comfortable with the change. Yes _____   No _____

The decision came easily. Yes _____   No _____

Two risks I've taken: _____

_____

_____

What motivated me to take the risks: _____

_____

_____

How my perception of the risks affected my decision:

1. _____

_____

_____

2. _____

_____

_____

Other risks I've taken in my life and career are _____

_____

_____

_____

I would describe my risk-taking style as _____

_____

_____

Managing Time

Planning a new career direction, exploring different occupations, and looking for work all require extra time and energy. For many of us, the time must be carved out of an already busy schedule. How well you manage your time affects your

How well you manage your time affects your career planning and your performance on the job.

Your Career and Life Plan Portfolio   © JIST Works

career planning and your performance on the job. Here are some questions you may want to consider:

- Am I satisfied with how I manage my time both on and off the job? If not, how can I improve my time-management skills?

- What keeps me from accomplishing the tasks that are important to me?

- Do I spend enough time on my high-priority activities?

 Tip If you are not satisfied with how you manage your time, meet deadlines, or accomplish your goals, many books and other resources are available on these topics. Ask your local librarian for suggestions.

The ability to achieve your goals on time or even ahead of schedule is a characteristic in high demand in today's workplace. But be aware that a good balance of work, home, and leisure activities offers the most satisfaction and helps reduce stress.

The following worksheet can help you understand your time-management style. Be sure to include any proof of your ability to meet goals on or ahead of schedule in your portfolio as well.

My Time-Management Style

I manage my time by _____

_____

_____

_____

_____

When faced with deadlines, I usually _____

_____

_____

One example in which I met a work-related goal ahead of schedule is _____

_____

_____

Dealing with Stress

Health factors can have a big impact on what you do with your life and what career you pursue. You can't control certain health conditions, but you can do something about stress. Prolonged stress has a negative effect on your body. It can even affect your body's ability to prevent illness.

> ### Tip
> Exercise your mind and body to relieve stress, to prevent illness, and to stay fit.

Change, especially change in career direction, is often stressful. In fact, changing jobs is one of the most stressful things you can do. Stress-management experts have found that people who lose a job or face an uncertain future tend to experience more health problems and have more accidents than usual.

Career-related stress often stems from a lack of job satisfaction. Of course, total job satisfaction is rare because there are disadvantages to every job. Yet knowing what these disadvantages are and how to deal with them is an important part of planning your career. If you are in a job that offers you no satisfaction (and a lot of stress), consider the following:

> Stress-management experts have found that people who lose a job or face an uncertain future tend to experience more health problems and have more accidents than usual.

- Do the disadvantages of your current position outweigh the advantages?

- Is there something you can do to change the situation?

- Is it likely the situation will change if you do nothing and wait it out?

- Is your attitude toward the situation likely to change?

- Why did you accept the position? Is it part of your long-term career plan?

Often, a situation appears hopeless until you step back and reevaluate it objectively. If you can't be objective, talk with people whose opinions you value and trust. Many resources are available to help you identify and deal with work-related stress.

> ### Tip
> Your ability to handle stress is another important consideration for employers as well, especially in jobs with strict deadlines or where numerous tasks are performed at once. If you are applying for such a job, be sure to include proof that you can meet deadlines and juggle multiple projects in your portfolio.

The following worksheet will show how vulnerable you are to stress. Evaluate yourself on each item. Refer to page 44 to score your responses.

How I Deal with Stress

1 = strongly disagree	**4** = slightly agree
2 = disagree	**5** = agree
3 = slightly disagree	**6** = strongly agree

I eat at least two balanced meals a day.	1	2	3	4	5	6
I get 7 to 8 hours of sleep each night.	1	2	3	4	5	6
I give and receive affection regularly.	1	2	3	4	5	6
I have several close relatives within 50 miles of my home on whom I can rely.	1	2	3	4	5	6
I exercise to the point of perspiration at least three times per week.	1	2	3	4	5	6
I seldom or never smoke.	1	2	3	4	5	6
I am the appropriate weight for my height.	1	2	3	4	5	6
I have an income adequate to meet basic expenses.	1	2	3	4	5	6
I get strength from my religious beliefs.	1	2	3	4	5	6
I regularly attend club or social activities.	1	2	3	4	5	6
I have fewer than three alcoholic drinks per week.	1	2	3	4	5	6
I have a strong network of friends and acquaintances.	1	2	3	4	5	6
I have several close friends I can confide in about personal matters.	1	2	3	4	5	6
I am in good health, including my eyes, ears, and teeth.	1	2	3	4	5	6
I am able to speak openly about my feelings when I'm angry or worried.	1	2	3	4	5	6
I have regular conversations with family members about problems, chores, money, and other daily-living issues.	1	2	3	4	5	6
I do something for fun at least once per week.	1	2	3	4	5	6
I am able to organize my time effectively.	1	2	3	4	5	6
I drink less than three cups of coffee, tea, and cola per day.	1	2	3	4	5	6
I take quiet time for myself during the day.	1	2	3	4	5	6

Total Stress Vulnerability Score = _____

Total Your Scores

If you have a score of **80 or more**, you generally have a low vulnerability to stress-related problems. However, looking for work can be more stressful than normal living. Take good care of yourself during your job search or career change.

If you have a score from **41 through 79**, you are moderately vulnerable to stress-related problems. A stress-management plan will be important during your job search. Design a plan and stick with it.

If you have a score of **40 or less**, you are highly vulnerable to stress-related problems. Examine the items that received the lowest scores and make some changes in your life. A stress-management plan will be critical to your physical and emotional well-being.

Staying Physically and Emotionally Healthy

People have various ways of coping with change and uncertainty. Some methods are more helpful than others. Eating well, exercising, and getting emotional support are effective ways of coping with change.

Taking care of your physical health helps relieve stress and enables you to manage life's changes successfully. Experts consistently emphasize the same two ways to stay healthy:

> Taking care of your physical health helps relieve stress and enables you to manage life's changes successfully.

- **Eat a balanced diet.** Machinery cannot operate without fuel. Similarly, your body cannot function well unless you provide it with a healthy, balanced diet. Your doctor or any nutrition expert at a local hospital or county health department can help you plan a healthy diet.

- **Exercise regularly.** Exercising produces helpful chemicals that ease tension, improve mood, and create feelings of well-being. Regular exercise helps your body ward off many illnesses, including those caused by stress. Keeping physically fit also helps you keep mentally fit. It's your best resource for keeping up with the rigorous demands of your career and life.

Your ability to deal with stress is also affected by your emotional health. Difficult times in your life are easier to handle if you don't try to handle them alone. If you are in the middle of a job search or a career change, you need an emotional support system. Various resources are available to provide job-seeking help, such as the following:

> Difficult times in your life are easier to handle if you don't try to handle them alone.

- Books or pamphlets that detail how to fill out job applications, write resumes or cover letters, and prepare for interviews. See the appendix for a list of some of these resources.

- Libraries or state employment services that can provide information about the local job market.

- Friends or family who can provide transportation, look over your resume, or care for your children while you go to an interview.

- People in the community who might know of possible job openings.

Some people describe changing careers or looking for work as being on an emotional roller coaster. Feelings of relief, sadness, anger, depression, hope, disappointment, and excitement are all normal under these circumstances. Regardless of the situation, most of us welcome the opportunity to talk about what we are going through. For emotional support, talk to people who will listen to your feelings, have a positive attitude, and believe in you and what you can do. Generally, no one person is able to provide all the support you need. Think about your current support network and how you might expand it.

 Tip Find a local career planning program or job club. You will meet people who have had experiences similar to yours and others who are trained to give emotional support and encouragement.

The following worksheet will help you think specifically about your strategy for staying physically and emotionally healthy.

My Physical and Emotional Health

I would describe my current physical health as _____
_____

My concerns about my physical health are _____
_____
_____

One thing I could do to improve my physical health is _____
_____
_____

I would describe my current emotional health as _____
_____
_____

My concerns about my emotional health are _____
_____
_____

One way my emotional support system could be improved is _____
_____
_____

Life Roles

The term *life roles* refers to the various parts you play in the story of your life. Your roles in life may include child, student, worker, parent, and partner, among others. The roles you assume teach you various skills, provide you with opportunities, and help you set priorities.

Life roles change. Sometimes you may be focused on only one role. At other times, you may be balancing several roles. As you plan your career, take into account the many roles you have had in the past, the roles you have now, and the roles you expect to have in the future. Think about what is important to you, your family, your background or culture, and your life.

> The roles you assume teach you various skills, provide you with opportunities, and help you set priorities.

Tip Don't limit your portfolio pieces to experiences drawn only from your role as an employee. Many of your possible experiences as a student, citizen, parent, coach, and volunteer contribute to your skills and make you attractive to employers. In your portfolio, try to include evidence of your personal and professional growth from many aspects of your life, not just your career.

The following worksheet will help you think about how your roles change. The first part of the worksheet is a list of roles you may now have. Not all the roles will apply to you, so just skip the ones that do not. Briefly describe each of your current roles. In the last part of the worksheet, list your past roles and probable future roles. The first part of the worksheet can give you some possibilities.

My Changing Life Roles

The check marks below indicate life roles I currently have. I've briefly described each of these roles.

_____ Student _____

_____ Spouse or partner _____

_____ Homemaker _____

_____ Parent _____

_____ Citizen _____

_____ Child _____

_____ Employer _____

_____ Employee _____

_____ Job seeker _____

_____ Volunteer _____

_____ Other _____

Roles I've had in the past: _____

_____

_____

Roles I expect to or would like to have in the future: _____

_____

_____

As you consider your career and life path, think about how you will balance all your roles. If you are thinking of returning to school or work, you will have to make room in your life for a new role. Think about how much time and energy each of your roles takes. Think about which of your life roles takes priority.

Many of your past and current life roles have provided you with skills and experiences you will need to succeed in your career. On the other hand, some roles may come into conflict with your career plans. Complete the following worksheet and consider how your life roles affect your career decisions.

My Life Roles and Career Decisions

Roles that give me experiences and help me develop the skills I need to make career changes:

_____
_____
_____

Roles that play a part in helping me reach my career goals:

_____
_____
_____

Roles that hinder my career planning:

_____
_____
_____

Changes I would like to make in the roles I now have:

_____
_____
_____
_____

Career Interests

Another key to career satisfaction is to find an occupation that interests you. Your local librarian can help you find books containing job descriptions. Such books provide information about each job's work environment, work activities, earnings, job outlook, skills required, and the education and training necessary to get the job.

One of the most widely used resources is the *Occupational Outlook Handbook*, which gives descriptions for more than 260 jobs based on data from the U.S. Department of Labor. You can find this handbook at your library or access its information online at www.bls.gov/oco. In addition, *Your Career and Life Plan Portfolio*'s appendix provides a list of additional resources you can use to identify and explore career interests.

 Tip Even if you don't have the necessary job qualifications now, don't reject an occupation you are truly interested in. Instead, look for ways to get the training you need.

After you have looked at a list of jobs, complete the following worksheet. In the left column, list jobs you could do with the skills and abilities you have now. In the right column, list jobs that interest you but that would require additional training, education, or experience.

Jobs That Interest Me

Jobs I could get with the skills and knowledge I have now

_____

_____

_____

_____

_____

Jobs that interest me but require additional training, education, or experience

_____

_____

_____

_____

_____

Another book, titled *New Guide for Occupational Exploration (GOE),* is also based on information from the U.S. Department of Labor and organizes jobs into 16 interest areas. For each job, the *GOE* provides information such as job duties, required level of training and education, average salary, projected growth, and necessary skills.

Read the descriptions of the 16 career areas on the following worksheet. Check any that interest you. Then rank the top three areas that interest you most (1, 2, and 3). You can then use the *GOE* or other career resources to find specific jobs within these interest areas.

Always keep your interests in mind as you look at career possibilities.

Always keep your interests in mind as you look at career possibilities. You also should consider areas that might interest you if you learned more about them.

My Career Interests

My main interests are in the following checked areas:

❑ **Agriculture and Natural Resources.** I have an interest in working with plants, animals, forests, or mineral resources for agriculture, horticulture, conservation, extraction, and other purposes.

❑ **Architecture and Construction.** I have an interest in designing, assembling, and maintaining components of buildings and other structures.

❑ **Arts and Communication.** I have an interest in creatively expressing feelings or ideas, in communicating news or information, or in performing.

❑ **Business and Administration.** I have an interest in making an organization run smoothly.

❑ **Education and Training.** I have an interest in helping people learn.

❑ **Finance and Insurance.** I have an interest in helping businesses and people be assured of a financially secure future.

❑ **Government and Public Administration.** I have an interest in helping a government agency serve the needs of the public.

❑ **Health Science.** I have an interest in helping people and animals be healthy.

❑ **Hospitality, Tourism, and Recreation.** I have an interest in catering to the wishes and needs of others so that they may enjoy a clean environment, good food and drink, comfortable accommodations, and recreation.

❑ **Human Service.** I have an interest in improving people's social, mental, emotional, or spiritual well-being.

❑ **Information Technology.** I have an interest in designing, developing, managing, and supporting information systems.

❑ **Law and Public Safety.** I have an interest in upholding people's rights or in protecting people and property by using authority, inspecting, or investigating.

❑ **Manufacturing.** I have an interest in processing materials into products or maintaining and repairing products by using machines or hand tools.

❑ **Retail and Wholesale Sales and Service.** I have an interest in bringing others to a particular point of view through personal persuasion and sales and promotional techniques.

❑ **Scientific Research, Engineering, and Mathematics.** I have an interest in discovering, collecting, and analyzing information about the natural world, life sciences, and human behavior.

❑ **Transportation, Distribution, and Logistics.** I have an interest in operations that move people or materials.

Documenting Your Goals, Values, and Personality

The information in this chapter is designed to give you a better sense of who you are, what matters most to you, and what you want out of your career and life. No single document in your portfolio can articulate these goals, values, and personality styles, but they are often expressed throughout the portfolio.

Such values, goals, and personality traits often find their way into personal statements and resumes and are usually reflected in awards, achievements, recommendations, and even samples of your work. By completing this chapter, you should be even more prepared to present these aspects of yourself through your portfolio.

> No single document in your portfolio can articulate these goals, values, and personality styles, but they are often expressed throughout the portfolio.

Tip Some professionals are expected to include a mission statement or some other kind of goals statement as part of their portfolios. For instance, educators often include a teaching philosophy in their portfolios. This brief (1–2 page) statement discusses the teacher's goals for the class and how he or she plans to achieve those goals. A mission statement can help an employer get a sense of who you are as a person, what you value in your life and your work, and what you hope to accomplish in the future.

Even more important than what might go in your employment portfolio, however, is how self-knowledge contributes to your career and life plan. Remember that the goal of this book is not just to help you get a job, but also to help you sort through career possibilities, help you manage the stress of your current life changes, and better prepare you for the changes to come.

Career and Life Plan Portfolio Checklist

Consider adding the following artifacts, documents, and resources to your master portfolio:

❏ A personal statement describing your career values and goals

❏ Proof to potential employers of your ability to learn quickly through whichever style fits you best

❏ Evidence of your decision-making and risk-taking styles

❏ Examples and other evidence that show your time-management skills

❏ Examples showing your abilities and accomplishments drawn from life roles outside work

❏ Records of any personality or values assessments you've taken

❏ Any information you've gathered from your initial career research

❏ Copies of any of the worksheets and exercises from this chapter that you'd like to keep as reference

▶ Let's Review

Complete the following checklist. Review information in this chapter that applies to any items you are unable to check.

End of Chapter Checklist

❏ I can describe what I value in my life and in my career.

❏ I know what my preferred style of learning is.

❏ I can describe my personality traits.

❏ I know how to make decisions.

❏ I know what my risk-taking style is, and I know how it affects the decisions I make.

❏ I am able to manage my time effectively.

❏ I know some steps to take in dealing with stress.

❏ I understand how to manage my physical and emotional well-being.

❏ I can identify my past, current, and future life roles, and I know how they affect my career planning.

❏ I know what type of work interests me most.

Date: _____

Chapter 4

What You Have to Offer

In Chapter 3, you focused on understanding who you are. You considered what to include in your portfolio to document your values, your interests, and your personal goals and history. The next step is to think about what you have to offer an employer. This chapter will help you answer these questions:

- What work experience do I have that would be of interest to an employer?

- What experience have I acquired in nonwork activities?

- What have I accomplished in my life and work?

- What skills have I developed?

- What education and training have I received?

- What have other people said about my knowledge, skills, performance, and accomplishments?

While the worksheets in this chapter are for your reference only, most of what is discussed in the chapter will be represented in your portfolio in one form or another. In fact, throughout the chapter you will be given suggestions for possible documents to include that will exhibit the skills, training, and experience you have to offer. As you complete each section, we urge you to consider how you can best prove your value to an employer and to gather any resources that you think might help.

Work History

There is little question that your work history plays an important role in an employer's decision to hire you. Likewise, it plays a prominent role in your portfolio, often comprising one of the largest sections. As you build your portfolio, however, you may think that the only work to take into account is your paid employment. If so, you underestimate what you have to offer. As you might have discovered in the preceding chapter, you have developed skills and built experiences in every part of your life.

> You have developed skills and built experiences in every part of your life.

Paid Employment

Your paid employment history is one of the most important considerations for a potential employer, which is why it finds its way onto your resume in one form or another.

For each of your current and past jobs, complete the following worksheet with information about your employer and your job description (feel free to make as many copies as necessary). Write as much about your job duties as possible. This will help you decide which tasks were your most important.

> **Tip** Employers prefer to talk to people who know what you can do and who have worked with you. Coworkers, former employers, and others who have firsthand knowledge of your skills and strengths can be valuable references. Be sure to ask people in advance if they will serve as references.

You can use the completed worksheets to help you write your resume, but you can also include the worksheets in your portfolio for reference. You can then refer to them when you are filling out job applications or talking to an employer.

My Paid Employment

Job title: _____

Name of employer/organization/contact person: _____

_____

Employer's phone: _____ Employer's fax: _____

Employer's street address: _____

City/State/ZIP: _____

Dates employed: _____

Job duties: _____

_____

_____

Special skills learned or training received: _____

_____

Person who could provide a reference for me related to this job: _____

_____

Person's address: _____

_____

Person's phone/fax: _____ Person's e-mail: _____

Job title: _____

Name of employer/organization/contact person: _____

_____

Employer's phone: _____ Employer's fax: _____

Employer's street address: _____

City/State/ZIP: _____

Dates employed: _____

Job duties: _____

_____

_____

Special skills learned or training received: _____

_____

Person who could provide a reference for me related to this job: _____

_____

Person's address: _____

_____

Person's phone/fax: _____ Person's e-mail: _____

Nonwork Experience

Activities you do in your nonwork time are important clues in deciding on an occupation. They can enhance your employability as well. The activities you choose to do around your home, for your community, and for other people in your leisure time are things you *want* to do. Thus, they often indicate the kinds of work that you would be most interested in. These activities also help you develop skills you can use on the job.

In your portfolio, include examples, photographs, programs, or other materials that show what you've learned or accomplished by participating in these nonwork activities. Also consider letters of recommendation from community leaders whom you might have worked with on a volunteer basis. These materials will help present you as a well-rounded person with multiple interests and skills.

On the following worksheet, list your nonwork activities. Examples might include serving on a committee at your child's school, teaching a class at your church, participating in political functions, working with a youth sport team, or organizing community projects for your social club. Complete the statements and then circle those activities you could do for pay.

> In your portfolio, include examples, photographs, programs, or other materials that show what you've learned or accomplished by participating in nonwork activities.

My Nonwork Experience

I have been involved in many activities not related to work. Circled activities are those I think I could also do in a job.

At home, I do the following jobs:

_____

_____

_____

In my spare time, I do these activities:

_____

_____

_____

In my community, I am active in the following:

_____

_____

_____

Accomplishments

Throughout your life, you have done things that provided a sense of accomplishment. It could be something you did several years ago or something you did just yesterday. Your accomplishments may or may not have received recognition from others, but what you did mattered to you.

> **Tip** You gain greater satisfaction from doing work that lets you use your skills. Focus on what you have done that makes you proud.

Looking at these accomplishments can help you identify your skills. The skills you used in achieving your accomplishments are usually those you are good at and enjoy using. If you can identify these skills and use them in your current and future jobs, you have a better chance at a successful and satisfying career. In addition, focusing on your accomplishments will strengthen your self-confidence. Remember to include anything that documents these skills or shows them in action in your portfolio.

In all your accomplishments, look for the skills you have developed. For example:

- If you have helped your friends do something, you may have learned to work as part of a team, and you may have developed problem-solving skills.

- If you have raised a family, you have probably developed people skills and a sense of responsibility and dependability.

- If you run a household, you may know how to budget your money, stay organized, and manage your time.

- If you have taken steps to keep physically fit and healthy, you probably have high energy, discipline, and motivation.

As you complete the following worksheet, list your accomplishments and other activities that you are proud of. Consider all your life experiences, not just those specifically related to work.

My Accomplishments

Three things I've done at work that I am really proud of:

1. _____
_____
2. _____
_____
3. _____
_____

Three things I've done in nonwork activities that I am really proud of:

1. _____
_____
2. _____
_____
3. _____
_____

Remember to include in your portfolio any evidence of these accomplishments, including certificates, ribbons, newspaper clippings, and anything else that records your achievements.

Tip Employers want to hire individuals who take pride in their work and are eager to achieve. Do not be afraid to show what you've done by documenting your accomplishments in your portfolio.

Skills and Attributes

One of the most important things you can do before deciding on or changing your career is to identify all your skills and abilities. You can then emphasize your most valuable skills and communicate to employers not only what you have done but how you did it.

People in the middle of a job or career decision often think of their abilities and skills in terms of their job titles. People trying to find their first jobs worry that employers won't think they have skills because they have no previous work experience. The truth is that most skills are applicable to a wide variety of jobs. Skills that are developed in school, in the home, and in volunteer situations are often transferable to job situations. Many skills that are important to employers are those that relate to your personality and that make you a good worker.

In the book *The Quick Job Search: Seven Steps to Getting a Good Job in Less Time*, author Michael Farr identifies three types of skills:

- **Self-Management Skills:** These skills spring from your basic personality and your ability to adapt to new situations. They are an indication of the kind of worker you will be. Flexibility, friendliness, and punctuality are examples of self-management skills.

- **Transferable Skills:** These skills may be learned in one job but can be used in other jobs. Meeting deadlines, supervising people, and writing clearly are examples of transferable skills.

- **Job-Related Skills:** These are skills you must have to be able to do a particular job. Being able to pilot a plane, prepare a teaching plan, or interpret a heart monitor are examples of job-related skills.

Tip If you need additional help in identifying and documenting your skills, you can find resources at your local library or bookstore. Also, talk with friends and coworkers and ask them what they think your most valuable skills are.

Remember that a skill is simply something you can do well. You probably have hundreds of skills, not just a few. Also, remember that there is a difference between what you do and what you *can* do. Your skills will change over time, and some skills will develop faster than others.

You are also likely to change careers more than once in your lifetime. Your ability to transfer your skills and adapt to a new career is very important. People who understand and communicate their skills well make job and career changes more easily than people who do not.

> People who understand and communicate their skills well make job and career changes more easily than people who do not.

Providing evidence of your skills and abilities is one of the primary functions of a portfolio. After all, employers are looking for proof that you have developed and used these skills in the real world. The following table illustrates how you might document skills in your portfolio.

Skill	How I Demonstrate This Skill	What I Can Include in My Portfolio
Self-management	I'm always on time for work.	My annual review
Negotiation	I wrote a chores contract for my family.	Copy of the family contract
Organization	I planned and organized all the activities for my high school reunion.	Letters to other committee members, copy of reunion program listing my name
Diplomacy	I helped my company reduce customer complaints by more than 30 percent.	Copy of my proposal plan, letter of commendation from my supervisor
Work ethic	I was Employee of the Month after only 6 months at my new company.	Employee of the Month certificate

Refer to this table as you complete the following worksheet. Place check marks beside the skills you have. Think about how you have demonstrated those skills. Then think about what you can include in your portfolio that would document those skills.

My Skills: Demonstrated and Documented

Skill	How I Demonstrate This Skill	What I Can Include in My Portfolio
_____ Analysis		
_____ Budget management		
_____ Communication		
_____ Computer literacy		
_____ Cooperation		
_____ Creativity		
_____ Critical thinking		
_____ Decision making		
_____ Dependability		
_____ Flexibility		
_____ Initiative		
_____ Integrity/honesty		
_____ Leadership		
_____ Listening		
_____ Mathematics		
_____ Negotiation		
_____ Persistence		
_____ Problem solving		
_____ Reading		
_____ Responsibility		
_____ Self-esteem		
_____ Self-management		
_____ Speaking		
_____ Teamwork		
_____ Tolerance		
_____ Other		

Education and Training

Your education and training act as an admissions ticket to be considered for a job. Certain career paths require certain levels of education. Other careers may have specific certification or licensing requirements. Some careers require you to take and pass national board exams. It is important to consider the educational requirements for a career as you explore your options.

Of course, it is equally important not to dismiss a career just because it requires more education and training than you currently have. Often the additional time and money required to get more education is worth the expense.

> Your education and training history is more than just a minimum requirement for a job. You learn many of your most valuable skills and gain valuable knowledge through your education and training.

In fact, many employers encourage their employees to continue their educations throughout their work lives. This is known as *lifelong learning*, and it is a growing expectation among employers, so much so that many employers offer tuition reimbursement plans to workers who further their formal educations. Be sure to ask your current or future employer about its tuition reimbursement policy.

Your education and training history is more than just a minimum requirement for a job. You learn many of your most valuable skills and gain valuable knowledge through your education. Your education—and your achievements during the course of that education—is an important source of your ability and probably has provided much of your career and life direction so far.

Because many employers will ask about it and may even expect evidence of it, having an Education and Training section in your portfolio helps. The following documents and information are examples of what you might include:

- Apprenticeships
- Certificates
- Continuing Education Units (CEUs)
- Courses completed
- Diplomas
- Favorite school subjects
- General Educational Development (GED) certificate
- Internships
- Languages
- Licenses
- Military training
- On-the-job training

- Scholarships
- Transcripts
- Volunteer service
- Workshops

Documentation also could be any material or stories from your life that show what you've learned. This might include what you have done on the job or in your home or community. It might be something you did just for yourself. Your portfolio is a good place to keep this material.

> **Tip** Be sure to make copies of transcripts, licenses, certificates, and diplomas to include if you plan to hand out your portfolio or leave it with an employer. If something should happen to it, you wouldn't want your originals lost or destroyed.

Testimonials and Recommendations

As you review your work and education experiences, remember to include in your portfolio any commendations; awards; letters of recognition; performance evaluations; and positive comments by supervisors, coworkers, customers, or clients.

You may hesitate to include recommendations in your portfolio for fear that you may appear conceited. But a portfolio is meant to provide the best possible picture of you. Anyone who looks at your portfolio will expect a record of your accomplishments, including positive feedback from others.

> **Tip** Most people do not want to brag about what they've done. However, remember that it's okay to share the positive feedback you have received from other people.

Keep any documents you have that indicate you have done something that made a difference in someone's work or life. If you have a lot of material for this section, however, be selective in what you show to employers. While you are expected to brag, including 20 letters of recommendation may start to look self-indulgent.

Use the following worksheet to organize and summarize the positive feedback others have given you. After Document, write the kind of testimonial it is—whether it's a letter of recognition, an evaluation, a customer feedback form, a certificate, etc. Next to Summary, write down the key skills, abilities, and values that this other person emphasizes and appreciates about your work. This will not only help you organize your portfolio but can help you know what to emphasize in an interview or on a resume as well.

Testimonials and Recommendations
Summary Sheet

Document: _____

Summary: _____

_____

_____

Document: _____

Summary: _____

_____

_____

Document: _____

Summary: _____

_____

_____

By this point, you should have a good sense of the kinds of materials to include in your portfolio. You should be able to document your interests, values, abilities, and skills. You should have an idea of what documents to include to reflect your past accomplishments, current abilities, and future aspirations. The remaining chapters will help you use this information to outline a career and life plan, rounding out your portfolio in the process.

Career and Life Plan Portfolio Checklist

Consider adding the following artifacts, documents, and resources to your master portfolio:

- ❏ A complete history of your paid employment, complete with references
- ❏ Documents showing nonwork experiences that have taught you valuable skills
- ❏ Proof of your accomplishments both inside and outside of work
- ❏ Documents, images, and artifacts that demonstrate your skills, including any examples or samples of your work
- ❏ Documents that show what you learned and accomplished through your education and training experiences
- ❏ Copies of recommendations, testimonials, or other positive feedback you've received

▶ Let's Review

Complete the following checklist. Review information in this chapter that applies to any items you are unable to check.

End of Chapter Checklist

- ❏ I have gathered information about my work experience.
- ❏ I can identify experience I have gained through my home, leisure, and community activities.
- ❏ I can identify my achievements related to work, learning, and leisure.
- ❏ I can explain the different types of skills.
- ❏ I have thought about the skills I have and how I demonstrated those skills in the past.
- ❏ I know what items to include in my portfolio to document my skills and abilities.
- ❏ I have several ideas about what to include in the Education and Training section of my portfolio.
- ❏ I have several ideas about what to include in the Testimonials and Recommendations section of my portfolio.

Date: _____

Part Three

Reaching Your Career Goals

"One of the great paradoxes of human development is that we are required to make crucial choices (about careers and work) before we have the knowledge, judgment, and self-understanding to choose wisely. Yet if we put off these choices until we feel truly ready, the delay may produce other and greater costs."

—Daniel J. Levinson,
The Seasons of a Man's Life

Chapter 5

Deciding on a Career Path

In previous chapters of this book, you learned what a portfolio is and how to organize it. You also bettered your understanding of who you are and what you have to offer an employer. In fact, you have probably collected most of the information you will include in your portfolio.

Now it's time to use some of that information to explore your career options and decide on a path. This chapter will help you answer the following questions:

- How do I cope with life changes and overcome personal barriers?

- What is my idea of the perfect job?

- How can I keep track of information I've researched about careers?

- What are some sources I can rely on for general career information?

- What are some sources I can turn to for information about specific careers?

- What options are available to me for getting additional training or education?

- Do I have what it takes to be self-employed?

- What occupations most closely match my idea of the perfect job?

- What one career option do I want to pursue now?

Most of the worksheets and checklists in this chapter are for your own personal reference; they should not be shown to an employer as part of your employment portfolio. However, the career options you explore and ultimately decide to pursue *will* dictate what goes into your portfolio. In addition, the information you gather about potential careers will help in your job search. It can be stored as part of your master portfolio for easy reference.

Life Changes

One sure fact of life is that little is certain. You have undoubtedly experienced and managed many changes in your life. These changes might include leaving home, having children, or entering into a new relationship. Because changes in careers make up such a big part of our lives and our identity, they rank as one of the most important, and most stressful, life changes around.

Many people do not like change. It means letting go of the familiar and moving toward the unknown. However, it is possible to think of change as a challenge. If you want to improve your work or situation, you will have to make some changes.

Overcoming Fear

Fear often accompanies change, regardless of the type—change in your career, schooling, location, or personal status. In her book *Dare to Change Your Job and Your Life*, author Carole Kanchier says this about fear:

> Fear often accompanies change. By identifying your fears, you can deal with them openly and honestly.

"Fears can be barriers to your progress. Growing, which is really just a matter of abandoning a comfortable position, usually involves pain. Trying to avoid pain by constructing rigid roles, defenses, viewpoints, or excuses only makes the process more difficult. The first and most important risk you can take is to be honest with yourself. Acknowledge your fears."

By identifying your fears, you can deal with them openly and honestly. All of us can learn to face change without fear. Taking action to overcome your barriers is the first step. Use the following worksheet to help you think about the changes in your life and how you handle such changes.

Dealing with Change

Two things I fear or dislike about change:

1. _____
_____
2. _____
_____

Two things that excite me about change:

1. _____
_____
2. _____
_____

Two things I have learned about myself from the changes I've faced:

1. _____
_____
2. _____
_____

Overcoming Barriers

When we succeed at something, we gain more confidence to push onward. You have probably accomplished many things on the job and in nonwork activities. As an adult, you also recognize that setbacks can and do occur. However, these setbacks can usually be overcome.

Life doesn't stand still. The economy changes. Industries and employment opportunities change. Jobs come and go. You can choose to stand still and be left behind, or you can choose to grow and pursue new opportunities. In part, the process of putting together your portfolio is a step forward in your personal growth, preparing you for the changes to come.

> Life doesn't stand still. You can choose to stand still and be left behind, or you can choose to grow and pursue new opportunities.

You may have circumstances in your life that hold you back from making the changes you want to make. These barriers prevent you from reaching a goal or fulfilling a dream. Creating your portfolio makes you aware of barriers you may be facing and helps you examine all the possibilities open to you.

You may feel that you are not free to make all the choices you would like to. You may feel that responsibilities, money, or other realities limit your options. Sometimes these circumstances can't be changed. If so, you have to make other choices. Often, however, you may be overlooking possibilities. You may be able to overcome a barrier if you think creatively.

If you feel that a barrier in your life keeps you from making the changes you want or from reaching your career goals, ask yourself the following questions:

- Is the barrier something I have built for myself, or is the situation really beyond my control?

- Can I change my way of thinking about the barrier?

- Are there ways around this barrier that I haven't considered?

On the following worksheet, place a check mark beside each item that is or could be a barrier for you. Briefly describe what you could do to overcome that barrier. For example, you may want to change jobs but don't have the educational background required for the job you want. To remove the barrier, you might have to sign up for evening classes and spread out your education over several years. Even if making this change takes time, you will eventually be able to improve your life and get the job you want.

My Personal Barriers

The items I've checked below are my personal barriers. I've described what I might be able to do to overcome each barrier I've checked.

_____ Transportation _____
_____
_____

_____ Money/Finances _____
_____
_____

_____ Education _____
_____
_____

_____ Appearance/Clothing _____
_____
_____

_____ Family responsibilities _____
_____
_____
_____

_____ Location _____
_____
_____

_____ Other _____
_____
_____

You now have a list of ideas about what you can do to remove the barriers in your life. Ask other people to help you expand your list. When you think your list is complete, pick one or two ideas and try them.

If you think your barriers are too great for you to overcome by yourself, seek out professional counselors who can help you. Don't expect to change your life all at once. Trying to make too many changes at one time can be overwhelming.

The Perfect Job for You

Changing jobs or careers can be difficult, but the more you plan for the change, the easier it will be.

Before you begin looking at career options, think about what your ideal job would be like. Think about the job that you've always wanted or that would meet most of your needs. Also consider what you know about yourself. Use the information you gathered in Chapter 3 to guide you.

> The more you focus on what you want, the closer you will get to finding your ideal job.

Few people work in an occupation that is ideal in every way. But the more you focus on what you want, the closer you will get to finding your ideal job. As you complete the following worksheet, imagine yourself in your perfect job.

My Perfect Job

Location and Environment

In my perfect job, I would stay in the United States. ❏ yes ❏ no

The region of the country I would work in is _____

The size of city I would work in is _____

I would work in ❏ an urban setting ❏ a rural setting

In my ideal job I would work ❏ inside ❏ outside

I would work for ❏ a big company ❏ a midsize company ❏ a small company

I would ❏ stay in one place ❏ move around

In my ideal job I would want to dress in _____

_____

My ideal job would reasonably pay me _____

Tasks and Responsibilities

My ideal job would mostly involve ❏ physical tasks ❏ mental tasks

My ideal job would primarily have me working with ❏ people ❏ data
❏ things ❏ ideas

I would be ❏ a leader ❏ a follower

I would be ❏ a planner ❏ a doer

The skills I would use in my ideal job are _____

_____

During a typical work day, I would _____

_____

Coworker Relations

In my ideal job, I would have a boss who is _____

_____

I would be the boss or supervisor. ❏ yes ❏ no

I would be part of a team. ❏ yes ❏ no

My coworkers in my ideal job could be described as _____

_____

I would primarily work alone. ❏ yes ❏ no

Gather Career Information

Whether you are looking for your first job, trying to move up in a company, or making a complete career change, you need to explore the labor market. The world of work changes rapidly, and understanding those changes can help bring you closer to that perfect job.

Through research, you can better evaluate the positive and negative aspects of various careers. You can then weigh these against your own values and needs. (Again, the information you gathered in Chapter 3 will help with this process.) When exploring careers, be sure to gather the following key information about specific jobs:

- The nature of the work
- The industries that include these occupations
- Training or education required
- Working conditions
- Potential earnings
- Employment trends and advancement possibilities
- Related occupations
- How well your values, interests, education, skills, and abilities match

In addition to specific jobs, you can research the labor market in general to learn about national, state, and local employment trends; occupations and industries that are growing or declining; and the current or anticipated job openings for a given industry.

Be sure to refer to several sources of information and look into a number of possibilities. As you move through your career exploration, use the following worksheet to keep track of your research. Feel free to make a photocopy of the worksheet for each occupation that interests you.

Through research, you can better evaluate the positive and negative aspects of various careers. You can then weigh these against your own values and needs.

My Career Research

Name of occupation: _____

Source of information: _____

Tasks, responsibilities, risks, and physical demands of this occupation: _____
_____
_____

Skills required to do this job (circle those skills you already possess): _____
_____
_____

Working conditions for this job (what kind of environment would you work in): _____
_____
_____

Work schedule (number of hours and days per week): _____
_____

Training, education, or other qualifications (degrees, licenses, registration, certification) required for this job: _____
_____
_____

Salary range for this job: _____

Employment outlook for the future of this occupation: _____
_____

Possibilities for advancement or promotion: _____
_____

Related occupations: _____
_____
_____

Sources of additional information (books, schools, people, Web sites): _____
_____
_____

Sources of Career Information

As you research career options, you may feel overloaded with information about jobs, industries, and opportunities. Newspapers, magazines, books, television, radio, the Internet, and friends all provide tidbits of information about career opportunities. But before relying on any source of career-related information, ask yourself these questions:

- Is the information up-to-date? Career information rapidly becomes obsolete.

- Is the information accurate and unbiased? Information passes through many sources and may be slanted or misinterpreted. Always consider the source.

- Is the information confirmed by other sources? Another way to judge information involves seeing, hearing, and reading the information in many sources. For example, if five different sources give you the same information about a career, you can probably rely on that information.

Do not disregard a career path or job prospect because you uncover some negative information. Continue exploring until you are satisfied you have all the information you need. Then you can make an informed and responsible decision. Remember, trust your own judgment above all else. The following sections describe tools you can use to explore your career options further.

> Continue exploring until you are satisfied you have all the information you need. Then you can make an informed and responsible decision.

Informational Interviews

The purpose of an informational interview is to gain information, *not* to interview for a job opening. Request an informational interview with someone who works in a career area that interests you.

The following list gives examples of informational interview questions. Design and add your own questions to ensure that you walk away from the interview with the information you need. Be sensitive and do not ask questions the person might find too personal. For example, specific questions about salary are usually not appropriate.

> The purpose of an informational interview is to gain information, *not* to interview for a job opening.

My Informational Interviews

General Questions to Ask

Preparation

- What credentials or degrees are required for entry into this kind of work?
- What types of prior experience are absolutely essential?
- How did you prepare for this kind of work?

Present Job

- What do you do during a typical work week?
- What skills or talents are most essential for effective performance in this job?
- How would you describe your work environment?
- What is the general pay range for this type of work?
- What are the toughest problems you deal with on a day-to-day basis?
- What do you find most rewarding about this job?

Life Style

- What obligations does your work put on your personal time?
- How much flexibility do you have in terms of dress, hours of work, vacation schedule, and place of residence?
- How often do people in your line of work change jobs?

Career Future and Alternatives

- If things develop as you would like, what career goals would you like to achieve?
- How rapidly is your present career field growing?
- How would you describe or estimate future prospects?
- If the work you do was suddenly eliminated, what other type of work do you feel you could do?
- What companies hire people with your background?

Job Hunting

- How do people find out about jobs in your career area? Are they advertised in the newspaper or professional journals? If so, which ones? Is the information sent out by word of mouth? If so, who spreads the word? Is the information sent out by your personnel department?
- How does a person move from one position to another in this type of work?

- If you were to hire someone to work with you, which of the following factors would be the most important in your hiring decision? Why?

    Educational credentials

    Personality, personal attributes

    Past work experience

    Applicant's knowledge of the organization and job

    Specific skills and talents

Advice

- How well suited is my background for this type of work?

- Can you suggest other related fields?

- What types of paid employment or other experience would you most strongly recommend?

- If you were just now entering the workforce, what would you do differently to prepare for this occupation? What coursework would you take? What kinds of practical experience would you try to get?

Referral to Others

- Based on our conversation today, can you suggest other people who can provide me with additional information?

- Can you suggest a few people who might be willing to see me?

- May I use your name when I contact the people you suggest?

Job-Specific Questions to Ask

If you determine during the interview that you might be interested in working for the same organization as the person you are interviewing, consider asking the following questions:

- What does your organization do?

- What is the size of your organization?

- What is the average length of time employees stay with the organization?

- How much freedom is given to new employees?

- What types of formal or on-the-job training does the organization provide?

- How often are performance reviews given?

- How much decision-making authority is given to an employee after 1 year?

- What new product lines or services is the company developing?

- How does the organization compare to its competition?

Job Shadowing

When you job shadow, you go to work with someone for a day, a few days, or even a week to observe all aspects of the person's work. This is an excellent method for seeing firsthand what a person in a job really does. Feel free to ask lots of questions, but don't get in the way (after all, you never trip over *your* shadow).

Job Clubs

You can find job clubs in community organizations, government agencies, outplacement firms, or schools. These programs train job seekers in how to look for work and how to locate and contact employers. A job club also provides practical help, such as a base for job hunting, employer listings, and office equipment. Program leaders and other job seekers provide structure, emotional support, and encouragement.

> Job clubs train job seekers in how to look for work and how to locate and contact employers. They also provide structure, emotional support, and encouragement.

Career Information Systems

Computerized career information systems may be available within your local community. Contact your library, nearby high school or college, or state employment office for this service. Many systems match information about you to possible occupations. Some systems provide job information such as work descriptions, skills required, training or education required, pay ranges, and related jobs.

Career Resource Centers

Career resource centers gather many sources of information in one place. They may be located in large businesses, schools, colleges and universities, libraries, or government or community agencies. Information may be in the form of books, journal articles, microfiche, video- and audiotapes, CD-ROMs, and Internet-based programs. Many resource centers have staff available to help you.

Outplacement Centers

These services often share information about job openings and employer lists. They may also provide resume-writing assistance, interview training, or career coaching.

The Internet

The Internet provides a huge amount of information about employment opportunities, career paths, education opportunities, and strategies for conducting a job search. Many sites provide career coaching, resume-writing assistance, and career-oriented tests and assessments. Other sites specialize in providing job descriptions and assisting in career research. Be aware that some Web sites provide inaccurate or misleading information, and others may charge fees for their services.

For general career exploration, start with government sites such as http://online.onetcenter.org and www.bls.gov/oco/home.htm. For a more detailed list of Internet resources, see the appendix in the back of this book.

Networking

Exploring career possibilities is simply a matter of making connections *(networking)* with people and sharing information. Studies have shown that networking is the best way to find a job. And it's not difficult to do. You already know many people. The people you know also know many people. These people are all part of your network.

> **Tip** To network effectively, you must tell people what you've done, what you do well, and what you want to do.

The purpose of networking is to share information that can lead you to a job. Your network can help you find out about various occupations and develop leads on interesting career options. Start with your family, friends, former employers, or coworkers. Also, talk with people you've met while volunteering in community activities or school organizations. They may know someone who could help you explore other career areas.

The following diagram illustrates a structured way of thinking about a network.

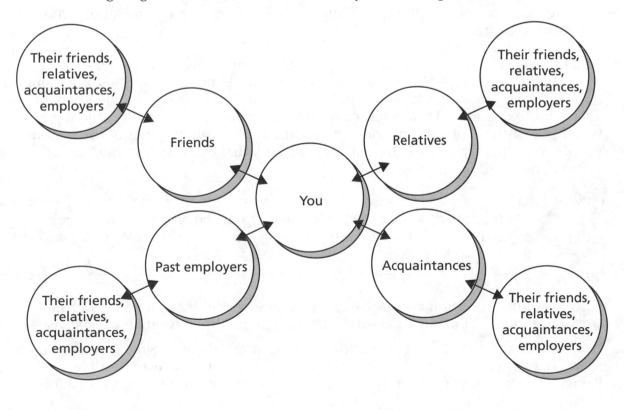

Many people you ask will tell you they don't know anyone who could help you. They're probably thinking only in terms of someone who could actually hire you. You have to be persistent and help the people in your network understand what you are after. A person may not be able to give you the name of an employer who will hire you, but he or she may give you the name of someone who can connect you to such a person.

> **Tip** Be sure to send a thank-you note for any information you receive from the people in your network.

When you network, start from a broad perspective. Memorize the following five "I" words to help you remember what you need to do:

- **Identify** what you want to do and what you do well. Determine what industry needs your skills and talents.

- **Investigate** available networking resources. Start with the people you know best and then branch out from there.

- **Initiate** a strategy. Use your resume as a brochure. Create your own business cards. Talk to people.

- **Imitate** people who are successful. Find out what works for them and how they got where they are. Follow in their footsteps.

- **Incorporate** and use all the information and resources you gather. Keep your perspective broad.

Expand your network by adding names and phone numbers of people you meet while exploring careers. When you talk with people about career options, ask them if they can recommend others who might help you. Ask each person you know to give you the names and phone numbers of three people who might be able to help you. Contact those people and ask them for the names and numbers of three more people. Very quickly you will have a large network that can help you find the information you need.

> **Tip** When you network, collect business cards, flyers, and brochures from people and businesses that interest you. Feel free to store these materials in your master portfolio for reference.

Once you find a position and are hired, make sure you let the people in your network know about your situation. Also be sure to thank them for their assistance.

Use the following worksheet to record information about your own network. Add more pages as you need them. Use actual names of people wherever possible. Remember, these people can help you discover career options now and find a job later.

My Network

Name: _____

Business or organization: _____

Phone number: _____ E-mail: _____

Address: _____

_____

How I know this person: _____

_____

Date(s) contacted: _____

Results of meeting/conversation: _____

_____

_____

Thank-you note sent? ❏ yes ❏ no

Name: _____

Business or organization: _____

Phone number: _____ E-mail: _____

Address: _____

_____

How I know this person: _____

_____

Date(s) contacted: _____

Results of meeting/conversation: _____

_____

_____

Thank-you note sent? ❏ yes ❏ no

Explore Training Options

Generally, the more education or training you have, the better your earnings and the more careers there are available to you. So getting qualified for a job that interests you may be well worth the extra time and money.

As you explore various occupations, don't exclude those that require more training or education than you currently have. Average earnings for college graduates are considerably higher than for those without college degrees. Consider the earnings impact of higher education as you look at jobs. Here are some sources of information about education and training options:

> As you explore various occupations, don't exclude those that require more training or education than you currently have.

- Adult education programs
- Apprenticeship councils
- Armed forces processing centers
- High school guidance offices
- Human resources departments
- Job training offices
- Local colleges or universities
- State employment offices
- Technical colleges
- Veteran's services centers
- Women's centers

In the future, most jobs will require some education or technical training beyond high school, and the fastest-growing jobs require at least a 2-year degree. As a result, many adults are returning to school for specialized training. As you gather information about education or training options, keep the following ideas in mind:

- **Get the employer's viewpoint.** Employers sometimes recruit from certain training programs and not others. If you are considering more education or training for a particular career, talk with employers before you enroll.

- **Comparison shop.** Just as tuition and fees vary from one school to another, so does the quality of the training. Call a number of programs to compare the quality and cost. Consider the time of day classes are held and length of the program. Ask if you can get credit for work experience and whether you can take courses by correspondence or other means.

- **Find out about accreditation.** Most schools (public or private, college or university, trade or technical) are certified by a national organization. Ask if the school is accredited and, if so, by what organization.

- **Ask about financial aid or tuition assistance.** Most schools have financial aid programs, and special programs in your area may provide funds for training. Find out whether you qualify. If you are currently working, your place of employment may help pay for additional training or education.

The following worksheet lists ways to upgrade your knowledge and training. Check those you are interested in pursuing. Use your network, the library, or high school or community college counseling offices to find out what training programs are offered in your area.

My Possible Training Options

I could get more training by...	Where	When
❏ Reading journals or books	_____	_____
❏ Attending workshops	_____	_____
❏ Beginning an apprenticeship program	_____	_____
❏ Beginning a job-training program	_____	_____
❏ Enrolling in a trade, technical, or vocational school	_____	_____
❏ Enrolling in a degree program		
❏ 2-year program	_____	_____
❏ 4-year program	_____	_____
❏ Master's program	_____	_____
❏ Other degree program	_____	_____
❏ Enrolling in informal courses	_____	_____
❏ Enrolling in company-sponsored courses	_____	_____
❏ Getting a license or certificate	_____	_____
❏ Joining the military	_____	_____
❏ Taking a temporary job that would add to my skills	_____	_____

Self-Employment

Small-business startups comprise one of the fastest-growing segments of our economy. They often take the form of self-employment. One of the best things about self-employment is that *you* define what success means, based largely on your reasons for wanting to start your own business. Most people find a certain satisfaction in turning their self-employment dream into something real.

> One of the best things about self-employment is that *you* define what success means.

Owning and running your own business calls for different skills than working for someone else. You can acquire the necessary skills and knowledge by attending classes on how to set up a small business. Some of what it takes to succeed in a small business depends on your abilities, personal management skills, and available resources as well.

If you want to pursue self-employment, research all options carefully. Three main ways to become self-employed are to start a new business based on your own idea, to purchase an existing business from someone else, or to buy a franchise. Before starting your own business, you might want to work for someone else in your chosen field. By doing so, you can acquire the necessary skills and experiences.

Many resources are available to help individuals become self-employed: chambers of commerce, economic development agencies, small-business development centers, and public libraries. In addition, you should talk to other small-business owners about their experiences, problems, mistakes, and successes. Add these people to your network, and keep any information they give you in your portfolio as well.

Tip Because one in three new businesses fails within 6 months, proper planning is key. A thorough business plan that addresses financing, marketing, and expanding your operation is a must.

The following worksheet lists attributes that might indicate you would do well working for yourself. If you find that many of the statements apply to you, perhaps you should explore starting a business (becoming an entrepreneur) or providing a service using your special skills (becoming a freelancer).

My Self-Employment Checklist

The checked statements apply to me.

_____ I have a great idea for a new product or service.

_____ I don't mind taking financial risks.

_____ I like to work hard on projects I believe in.

_____ I like being in charge of things and taking all the responsibility for success and failure.

_____ I am creative, flexible, and open to new ideas.

_____ I am a self-starter, with a lot of self-discipline.

_____ I can commit myself 100 percent to meeting deadlines.

_____ I like working alone.

_____ I have financial management skills.

_____ I like setting my own schedule.

_____ I am able to motivate myself and others when I believe in what I am doing.

_____ I work well with others even if I have just met them.

_____ I am able to convince others to adopt my point of view.

My business idea(s): _____

_____

_____

_____

_____

Decide on a Career Direction

People make career decisions in various ways. Some choose careers based on the advice of others. Some take the first job that comes along. Many working adults say they would choose differently if they could do it over again—and they would definitely get more information before making a decision.

You, on the other hand, have spent considerable time thinking about who you are and what you want. Once you gather information about career possibilities, you are ready to review your choices and make some decisions. Use the information you've already gathered for your portfolio to help you decide.

> Once you gather information about career possibilities, you are ready to review your choices and make some decisions.

Career Decision-Making Model

Making satisfying decisions is a learning process; there is no magic formula. But there are ways to organize your thoughts and feelings to help you make sensible choices. The following model traces the basic steps to take when making decisions.

You completed the first two steps in previous chapters. You already have a good idea about who you are and what options are available to you. You've explored potential careers and identified your ideal job. Now it's time to weigh your options and decide what you want.

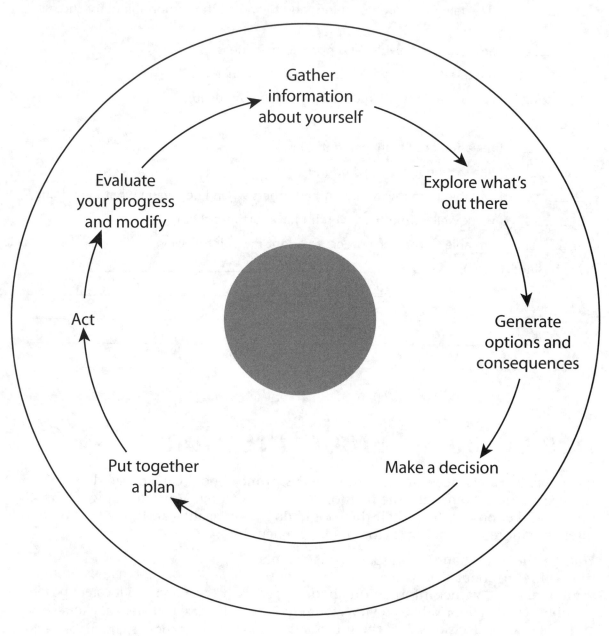

Decide to Decide

We all have a tendency to put off doing things. Sometimes we face conflicts. Sometimes we feel we just don't have the time. Sometimes we simply don't want to do them. Yet very few of us can afford to put off making a decision about our career.

There are no right or wrong reasons for wanting to make a career decision. Maybe you want more time to spend at home with your family or a position that pays more or offers more benefits. Maybe you want more long-term security or want to do work that benefits others. Just remember that no external factors can keep you from deciding to decide.

Evaluate Options and Consequences

Every action you take has consequences. You cannot predict every consequence for every action, and many consequences are beyond your control. The key to positive consequences is to think before you act, to anticipate the outcome of your actions. One way to do that is to learn as much as you can about the action you are considering.

> Every action you take has consequences. The key to positive consequences is to think before you act.

Remember that, in every situation, you have control of your own attitudes and reactions. You also have at least some control over your circumstances. If you have completed the exercises in this book, you are armed with the knowledge to make better choices, which will result in better consequences.

> Remember that in every situation you do have control of your own attitudes and reactions.

You most likely have discovered by now that you have many choices and options. One of the most difficult parts of decision making is sorting out and narrowing your options. The following Career Options Grid can help.

Career Options Grid

The key to identifying your best options is to compare information about yourself to information about career possibilities. You may be considering new career options, or you may want to move your current career in a new direction. Perhaps you have decided you want to stay in the same occupation but consider a new job. As you complete the following worksheet, ask yourself these questions about your career options (and use the information you've gathered for your portfolio to help you):

- Does this career option involve tasks and responsibilities that interest me?

- Does it require the skills I have or would like to develop?

- Is the work schedule and environment suitable for me?

- Do I have the required training or education?

- Will this career option provide an adequate income for me?

- What is the overall job outlook for this career option?

- Does this career option match my values, temperament, and the amount of risk I want to take?

- Do I have disabilities that would get in the way of doing the work?

- How does this career option fit in with what I picture for my future?

Look at the following worksheet. Here's how the grid works:

1. Down the left side of the grid are work and personal characteristics.

2. The first column at the top is labeled "Ideal Job." In this column, every work and personal characteristic is checked, because your *ideal* job would meet each of these requirements.

3. In the other columns across the top, list career options you are considering in the spaces provided.

4. In the column below each career option, check the characteristics that the option has in common with your ideal job, as far as providing what you want.

5. Leave the space blank if the option doesn't fit.

My Career Options Grid

Work Characteristics	Ideal Job	Option 1:	Option 2:	Option 3:	Option 4:	Option 5:
Advancement	X					
Coworkers	X					
Earnings	X					
Location	X					
Outlook	X					
Physical demands	X					
Responsibilities	X					
Risks	X					
Tasks	X					
Work environment	X					
Workload	X					
Work pace	X					
Work schedule	X					

Personal Characteristics						
Accomplishments	X					
Career values	X					
Decision-making style	X					
Education and training	X					
Emotional health	X					
Life roles	X					
Life values	X					
Learning style	X					
Nonwork experience	X					
Personality style	X					
Physical health	X					
Risk-taking style	X					
Skills	X					
Stress-management style	X					
Time-management style	X					
Work experience	X					

Reviewing Your Career Options Grid

Review what you have checked under each career option. Rank your career options according to how well they match your work and personal characteristics. Judge what is most important to you. Are earnings more important than an agreeable work environment? Is having a good work schedule more important than getting to use your skills? Narrow your choices to the top two options.

Now consider what might happen if you choose one of those two careers to pursue. What might be the consequences of your decision? Can you live with those consequences? How would your decision change your life? Think of both positive and negative outcomes. Use the following worksheet to compare your top two career choices.

My Top Two Career Choices

Of the careers I've considered, two I think most closely match my idea of the perfect job:

1. _____

2. _____

Some possible positive and negative consequences of these two options:

1. _____
_____
_____
_____
_____

2. _____
_____
_____
_____
_____

Make a Decision

Making a decision is difficult. One common misconception is that there are good and bad decisions. In reality, there are only satisfying and unsatisfying decisions. And you are the only one who can determine whether your decisions are satisfying or unsatisfying.

Whatever you decide, make a commitment to that decision. Plan out how you will follow through on it. Sometimes breaking things down into a series of attainable goals produces a more realistic and clear picture. Commitment to making your decision a reality means being self-directed and focusing your energies on a new course of action.

Be aware of how you feel after you make your decision. Are you excited about the possibilities that await you? Are you afraid of the outcome? Are you just relieved to have made a decision—any decision? Are you confident that you made the best choice available?

> Whatever you decide, make a commitment to that decision. Plan out how you will follow through on it.

Remember that feeling apprehensive or scared doesn't mean you made the wrong choice. Those feelings are normal reactions to change. However, if you are feeling more anxiety than contentment, you may want to go back through the decision-making process again.

Also, remember that no decision is final; you can always change your mind and revise your decision. Just be sure you stick with your decision long enough to objectively evaluate your progress and make necessary modifications. In time, you may feel perfectly comfortable with a decision that you felt anxious about at first.

In the following worksheet, choose the career option you will pursue. Record the reasons you think this is the best choice for you.

My Decision

Based on my Career Options Grid, the career I have chosen to pursue: _____
_____

My reasons for this decision: _____
_____
_____
_____
_____

My feelings about making this decision: _____
_____
_____
_____
_____

Congratulations. You now have a career path. Armed with your portfolio and the self-confidence that comes from knowing who you are, what you want, and what you have to offer, you are ready to take action. The final chapter will show you how.

Career and Life Plan Portfolio Checklist

Consider adding the following artifacts, documents, and resources to your master portfolio:

❏ A description of your ideal job

❏ Information on specific jobs you have researched and are interested in

❏ Notes you have gathered from informational interviews

❏ Business cards, flyers, and brochures from the people you've networked with

❏ Information gathered from career resource centers, job clubs, and outplacement centers

❏ Information about education and training options that you might be interested in pursuing, now and in the future

❏ Business plans and other documents that describe your ideas for starting your own business or doing freelance work

❏ A copy of your Career Options Grid for future reference

❏ An updated goals statement with your newly decided-upon career goal

► Let's Review

Complete the following checklist. Review information in this chapter that applies to any items you are unable to check.

End of Chapter Checklist

❏ I understand how to cope with change and have strategies in mind for overcoming personal barriers.

❏ I can identify what would be an ideal job for me.

❏ I am familiar with several sources of career information.

❏ I know what kinds of questions to ask in an informational interview.

❏ I understand the importance of finding and enlisting people to be in my network.

❏ I know how to record information I've found about careers I'm interested in.

❏ I can identify community resources that offer or support education and training.

❏ I can identify and use information resources that give me details about occupations.

❏ I know what skills are necessary for self-employment.

❏ I have compared several career options to my idea of the perfect job.

❏ I have chosen the two career options that most closely match my ideal job.

❏ I am aware of some possible positive and negative consequences of my career decisions.

❏ I have chosen the career option I will pursue at this time and can explain why I chose that option.

Date: _____

Chapter 6

Getting and Keeping Your Job

In the preceding chapter, you made a career decision. Now it's time to act on that decision. After all, that is the main goal of your portfolio: to help you get and keep your ideal job. In this chapter, you will put together a plan for landing a job in the career area that interests you most.

This chapter will help answer these questions:

- What actions do I need to take to make my dreams a reality?

- What tools and information will I need in my job search?

- When I am offered a job, how can I decide whether it's the right job for me?

- After I find a job, what can I do to help ensure that I keep my job and continue to improve as an employee?

- How does my portfolio contribute to both my job search and my continued career success?

When you complete this chapter, you will have the confidence and knowledge necessary for finding and keeping a job. You will also have finished gathering what you need for your portfolio and will be ready to use it to convince an employer to hire you. In short, you will be prepared to put your career and life plan in motion.

Put Together a Plan

Once you've made your decision, it's time to *do* something about that decision. Many methods can help you find a job, but your success ultimately depends on how much time and energy you are willing to invest in your search. Keep in mind that there is no *best* way to find a job. The best way is the way that works for you.

On the worksheet that follows, write your goal and list what you must do to accomplish it. Give yourself a deadline for each step. What do you need to do today, tomorrow, next week? Make your deadlines reasonable, but don't allow yourself time to get sidetracked. After writing down the steps and dates, sign your plan and date it.

> Keep in mind that there is no best way to find a job. The best way is the way that works for you.

Next, share your completed worksheet with someone else. This is a way of making the commitment to carry out the steps and keep yourself on schedule. Find someone who will be supportive of your plans. Tell this person about your deadlines and ask him or her to check with you on your progress. You may want to have this person sign and date the worksheet as well. Knowing that someone will be monitoring your progress motivates you to get things done.

Check your plan often as a reminder. Use another sheet of paper if you need more space.

My Plan of Action

My goal: _____

_____

_____

I will take the following steps to reach this goal:

First step: _____ Deadline date: _____

Second step: _____ Deadline date: _____

Third step: _____ Deadline date: _____

Fourth step:_____ Deadline date: _____

Fifth step: _____ Deadline date: _____

I understand that this is my plan and that I have a responsibility to complete it and to review and update it regularly.

Signature_____ Date _____

I have shared this plan with _____

Signature_____ Date _____

Take Action

Now that you have a plan, it's time to take action. The key to reaching your goal is to follow your plan and to modify and add to it as needed. Take the steps one at a time. A dream can become a reality, but it seldom happens overnight.

If your next step is to look for a job, you will need certain tools. The following sections describe some of those tools.

Job Applications

You will fill out applications before interviews or during the hiring process. Often, your job application gives employers their first look at you. How you fill out a job application reveals whether you have the following important characteristics:

1. **The ability to prepare and think ahead.** Secretaries and receptionists have many stories to tell about unprepared applicants who ask for pens, pencils, and telephone books. Having a copy of the following Job Application Fact Sheet in your portfolio will ensure you are prepared. Of course, your portfolio should include several copies of your resume as well.

2. **The ability to follow instructions and to convey information accurately.** Every job requires you to read, understand, and follow written instructions, rules, or procedures. Be sure you fill out the job application correctly.

> ***Tip*** Be honest. If you are hired for the job and your employer discovers that you have intentionally lied on the application, you will likely be fired.

3. **The ability to complete a document neatly and to follow through on a task.** Crossed-out or poorly erased information gives a negative impression. Be careful not to leave any sections or lines in the application blank. For these questions, write "N/A" (nonapplicable).

You can use the following worksheet to organize the information you need for filling out applications. Complete the form and take it with you as a reference when you fill out a job application or have an interview. If you have done the worksheets for other chapters, you've already gathered most of the information called for here.

My Job Application Fact Sheet

Identification

Name _____

Street address _____

City _____ State _____ ZIP _____

Phone _____ E-mail _____

Social Security number _____ Driver's license number _____

Name and telephone number of a person to contact in an emergency _____

_____

Type of job desired/Job requirements _____

_____

_____

Name of position I am applying for _____

Date available to begin work _____ Salary or pay rate expected _____

Previous Employment

Job title _____

Employer _____

Street address _____

City _____ State _____ ZIP _____

Phone _____ Fax _____

Dates employed _____ Reason for leaving _____

Special skills demonstrated _____

_____

Job title _____

Employer _____

Street address _____

City _____ State _____ ZIP _____

Phone _____ Fax _____

Dates employed _____ Reason for leaving _____

Special skills demonstrated _____

_____

Job title _____

Employer _____

(continued)

(continued)

Street address _____

City _____ State _____ ZIP _____

Phone _____ Fax _____

Dates employed _____ Reason for leaving _____

Special skills demonstrated _____

_____

Formal Education

School most recently attended _____

Address _____

Dates attended _____ Degree earned _____

Activities, honors, clubs, sports _____

_____

School _____

Address _____

Dates attended _____ Degree earned _____

Activities, honors, clubs, sports _____

_____

References

Name _____

Street address _____

City _____ State _____ ZIP _____

Phone _____ E-mail _____

Relationship (employer, teacher, coworker, clergy) _____

Name _____

Street address _____

City _____ State _____ ZIP _____

Phone _____ E-mail _____

Relationship (employer, teacher, coworker, clergy) _____

Name _____

Street address _____

City _____ State _____ ZIP _____

Phone _____ E-mail _____

Relationship (employer, teacher, coworker, clergy) _____

Resumes

A resume is a key component of your portfolio, acting as a summary of both the portfolio's contents and your life's work. Employers want more than a chronological list of job duties, however. They are interested in how well you did your job, what skills and experience you have to offer, and what you've accomplished. While your portfolio will answer these questions in more depth, your resume should provide the highlights.

> Employers want more than a chronological list of job duties. They want to know how well you did your job, what skills and experience you have to offer, and what you've accomplished.

Review the worksheets in previous chapters to identify information you want to include in your resume. Also, look through the other documents in your portfolio. Review educational records, training certificates, and letters of recommendation or performance evaluations for information you may want to include.

The goal of writing a resume is to include just enough information to get an interview. Save the detailed information for the portfolio and the interview itself. Think of a resume as an advertisement you use to get an employer interested in you.

Tip Some companies use hiring kiosks—computer terminals where you can sit down and fill out an application directly on-screen. If you use one of these, be sure to bring a copy of your resume and your Job Application Fact Sheet to make it easier to fill in the form.

Your resume should

- Be free of spelling, punctuation, grammar, or keyboard errors
- Be short, concise, and specific
- Be appealing to the eye and printed on quality paper
- Emphasize your accomplishments and how you can benefit the employer
- Highlight the skills and strengths you have that relate to your target job

Remember the following points as you put your resume together:

1. **The most effective resume is one that focuses on the requirements of the job.** Just as you may have more than one version of your portfolio, you may need two or three versions of your resume if you are applying for different kinds of jobs. Use the same basic information in each version of your resume, but arrange and emphasize your skills, abilities, strengths, and background information differently to match the requirements of each job.

   Another option is to customize your cover letter to list the most important information about you that matches each job's requirements.

2. **Your most important assets should be highlighted near the top of your resume.** The top half of the first page of your resume is referred to as the "prime space." This area should contain the information that is most important for the employer to see. You might want an employer to know about your current or most recent job or about your recent training. You might want the employer to have a summary of your education, experience, skills and strengths, or achievements. Choose what is most important for the particular job.

3. **Your name, address, and phone number should appear at the top of the resume.** Use bold lettering or divide the sections of your resume with lines to make it easier to read. You also may want to use bold type or underline the high points of your resume. This might include the names of the companies for which you have worked and your dates of employment. Bold or underlined type allows a prospective employer to skim the page and immediately see this information.

Tip Keep multiple copies of your resume in your portfolio so you can refer to it and hand it out as needed.

Use the following worksheet as a guide for assembling the essential elements of your resume. After you have the information together, try various formats until you have a design that is functional and agreeable. See the appendix for additional resources on creating effective resumes.

My Resume Worksheet

Name _____

Address _____

Telephone _____

E-mail _____

Summary

Here's a description of who I am, what industry knowledge I have, my marketable skills and attributes, and how I can benefit the company and employer: _____

_____

_____

_____

_____

The kind of position I want: _____

_____

_____

_____

Education and Training

My recent education and training: _____

_____

_____

_____

How this education and training match my job target: _____

_____

_____

_____

_____

Current or Most Recent Job

Description: _____

_____

List of skills: _____

_____

_____

_____

_____

List of achievements and outcomes: _____

_____

_____

_____

_____

Summary of experience: _____

_____

_____

_____

_____

Qualification Highlights

_____

_____

_____

_____

Previous Employment

_____

_____

_____

_____

Additional Education and Training

_____

_____

_____

_____

Cover Letters

In the past, most cover letters merely told the employer where the applicant had heard about the job and indicated that a resume was attached. Today's cover letters serve a variety of purposes, however. Mostly, like the portfolio, they provide yet another way for you to present the best version of yourself to employers.

> **Tip** If you send your resume with a cover letter that is hurriedly prepared and that contains even one conspicuous error, all your effort on your resume will be wasted.

When possible, your cover letter should

- Show a link between you and another person the employer already knows
- Describe your interest in the job
- Indicate your knowledge of the organization
- List additional information not included in your resume
- Emphasize your skills, background, and strengths and show how they match the job requirements
- Explain any special circumstances
- Indicate your interest in being interviewed
- Be free of spelling, punctuation, grammar, or keyboard errors
- Use a standard business letter format printed on quality paper
- Be addressed to a specific individual by name and title, if possible

Keep your cover letter short (one page) and make sure it is easy to read. Avoid long paragraphs. Use short lists. If you are unsure about proper spelling and grammar, refer to a dictionary. Ask someone who has good writing skills to proofread your letter.

> **Tip** Your cover letter is the perfect opportunity to deliver customized information to an employer. It draws attention to information you want to highlight in your resume and allows you to market yourself directly to a job description.

The following sample cover letter can serve as a guide for you as you write your own.

Sara N. Wrap
7 High Street
Haverhill, MA 01850
(978) 555-3745
saranwrap@aol.com

January 1, 20XX

Mr. Robert L. Smith
Vice President, Smith Industries
123 Market Street
Sellersburg, IN 11122

Dear Mr. Smith:

I am writing in regard to your Marketing Communications Manager position. As a professional with 5 years of experience in marketing, research, sales, and management, I know I would be a good fit for your company.

I am sure you will agree that my extensive and related experience makes me the ideal candidate to lead your marketing team. Highlights of my experience that specifically match the job include the following:

- Extensive experience developing marketing plans from concept to implementation to evaluation

- More than 10 years of experience doing direct marketing research and serving in a supervisory and analytical capacity

- Coordinated advertising and promotional campaigns for two Fortune 500 companies, developing the concepts and coordinating all resources

- Extensive firsthand knowledge of healthcare industry learned through previous employment

As requested, I have enclosed my resume with further details of my qualifications and accomplishments. A complete portfolio is available upon request. I look forward to meeting with you to discuss how I can add value to your marketing strategy. I will call you early next week to see if we might set a mutually convenient time to meet.

Sincerely,

Sara N. Wrap

Now use the following worksheet to compose your own personalized cover letter.

My Cover Letter Outline

(my name) _____

(street address) _____

(city, state, ZIP) _____

(phone number) _____

(other contact information) _____

(date) _____

(employer's name) _____

(employer's job title, company name) _____

(street address) _____

(city, state, ZIP) _____

Dear (employer's title and last name): _____

(paragraph stating what I know about the company or industry and telling the name of a referral if I have one) _____

_____

_____

_____

(general statement of what I know about the position and why I am well suited to the position) _____

_____

_____

_____

(more specific description of the skills, abilities, and strengths I bring to the position— bullet points or a paragraph) _____

_____

_____

_____

(concluding paragraph that states when and how I will follow up, requests an interview, and says thank you) _____

_____

_____

Sincerely,

(my signature) _____

(my printed name) _____

Employer Contacts

In Chapter 5, you learned about the importance of networking. One of the best ways to expand your network is to contact employers directly by phone or e-mail.

Many job seekers say that calling employers to ask for interviews can be daunting. If you are one of those people, having a telephone script can help. A script should include the following information:

- A greeting
- Your name
- The name of the contact person who suggested that you call

- The purpose of your call
- Two or three things about you that will interest the employer
- A request for a face-to-face meeting

Tip If you still find yourself uncomfortable calling a stranger about job openings, start by making one or more practice calls to people you know. This will prepare you for calling people you don't know.

Sometimes an employer insists on interviewing you over the phone. This is a good thing. Keep your portfolio handy to help you remember what you want to say about yourself. If you call an employer who decides to interview you on the phone, send the employer your resume and a thank-you letter as a follow-up. Of course, if you have a copy of your portfolio on CD, you should send it as well.

The following worksheet will help you develop a phone script. When you have completed this exercise, practice your script with others. Keep refining your script until the words come naturally. Also be sure your script is not too long; you need to get across all your vital information in the first 30 seconds or so.

My Telephone Script

Good morning. My name is _____

I'm calling at the suggestion of (name of referral) _____,
a business acquaintance of yours. He/she said you might know of an opening in your organization or another organization that needs a person with my abilities.

I have more than _____ years of experience in (description of the skills, abilities, and strengths I can contribute to the organization; information about how well I perform my tasks and responsibilities) _____

_____

_____

_____

When would be a good time for me to come in for an interview?

To conclude the phone call, always ask *when* you can come in for an interview, not *if* you can. Make it hard for the employer to turn you down. Consider keeping a copy of your phone script in your portfolio for reference.

Interviews

The more you prepare for an interview, the better you do. The two key steps to preparing for interviews are finding out about the employer and practicing answering interview questions.

Finding Out About the Employer

Employers like applicants who take the time to learn about the job and the company. By doing so, you let the employer know that you are highly interested in the job and are willing to do your homework. The background information you gather before the interview will also help you decide whether the job and organization are a good fit. This information is available through the following resources:

> Employers like applicants who take the time to learn about the job and the company.

- People in your network or people who work for the company where you will be interviewing

- Job postings

- Company brochures and Web sites (most companies have an "About Us" page that can be highly informative)

- The company's competition, vendors, and customers

- Reference materials in your local library, particularly periodicals

- Public or private placement services

Practicing the Interview

If you cannot communicate your skills and abilities to an employer, you probably will not get the job. Practice can help. Many employers ask standard questions in an interview. The questions generally fall into a few categories such as work history and experience, strengths and weaknesses, goals, education or training history, and how you fit the job and the organization.

> If you cannot communicate your skills and abilities to an employer, you probably will not get the job.

 Tip Practice in front of a mirror or with a friend who will give you good advice. If you can, find someone who has hiring and interviewing experience. This person can tell you what you're doing right and where you could improve.

Many books and government pamphlets on job seeking contain lists of frequently asked interview questions. Find a list and practice answering the questions. Spend more time on the ones that are hard to answer. Sometimes schools, colleges, or job training agencies have workshops on interviewing as well. See the appendix for more interview resources.

Here are some additional tips to remember:

- Arrive at the interview early.

- Be courteous and professional at all times.

- Know what is in your resume and bring extra copies along with your portfolio.

- Think about how you can solve the employer's problem and benefit the company.

- Use your portfolio to help you answer questions by pointing to specific examples and accomplishments.

- Go into the interview with a positive attitude.

- Give complete but concise answers to questions.

- Do not make negative comments about previous employers or coworkers.

- Keep your remarks targeted to the job. Sometimes even an interviewer gets off the subject, but try to remain focused on the matter at hand.

- Leave personal concerns at home so they do not hinder your chances.

- Do not bring up salary or compensation. Let the employer do that.

The questions on the following worksheet are ones employers frequently ask. Get ready for your next interview by answering these questions. You should also practice referencing key sections of your portfolio as you answer each question. For example, use documents from the Personal Goals and History section to help you answer the first question.

My Practice Interview Questions

Tell me something about yourself.

_____
_____
_____

Why are you interested in this job?

_____
_____

What kind of work have you been doing?

_____
_____

What would previous employers say about you?

_____
_____

What are your strongest skills, and how have you used them?

_____
_____
_____

What are your weaknesses, and what would you like to improve about yourself?

_____
_____
_____

What have you learned from previous jobs?

_____
_____
_____

What is your most significant work experience?

_____
_____
_____

Why should I hire you for this job?

_____
_____
_____
_____

The Interview and the Portfolio

A portfolio can be a valuable resource throughout the job search process, but its true power shows up in the interview. A portfolio with your awards and achievements, documents showcasing your skills and talents, and samples and evidence of your best work won't do you much good if nobody sees it.

Thus, your employment portfolio—those parts of your master portfolio that you intend to show to potential employers—should be with you at every interview. As you answer questions, be sure to point to supporting documents, references, and awards that prove your value. You can *tell* someone that you graduated in the top 10 percent of your class or that you were employee of the year, but having a copy of your transcript or a copy of the certificate you were awarded makes it more real.

> Your employability portfolio should be with you at every interview. As you answer questions, be sure to point to supporting documents, references, and awards that prove your value.

Follow Up

Most employers would rather give a job to someone who really wants it than to someone who does not seem to care. By following up after making a contact or having an interview, you show the employer how eager you are to get the job.

> By following up after making a contact or having an interview, you show the employer how eager you are to get the job.

Consider the following:

- You may be the only applicant who takes the time to write a follow-up letter or make a phone call.

- Your follow-up is an opportunity to tell the employer something you may have forgotten to mention in the interview.

- The employer may have several job openings. If you are not right for one, you may be right for another. Your follow-up gives an employer a reason to take another look at you.

- If the employer is not interested in you, always ask for the name of someone else you can contact for job leads. This will give you hope and may lead you to your next job.

- Always follow up within 24 hours after the interview.

Thank-You Notes

One of the most effective ways to follow up after a job interview is to send a thank-you note. Thank-you notes can be sent by regular mail or e-mail and should be short and to the point. In addition to showing your gratitude, be sure in your thank-you note to

- Use a formal salutation such as Dear Ms. Smith
- Very briefly remind the person of your skills and qualifications
- Set a date and time for following up
- Include information about how best to reach you

You can use the following sample to help you write your own thank-you notes

---

August 14, 20XX

Dear Mr. Jennings,

Thank you very much for the interview yesterday. I was most impressed with your company and everyone I met there. Working for a company such as yours would give me the chance to develop my sales and marketing skills even further and build on 8 years of experience I have in the field.

I will contact you within a week to answer any questions you may have. Feel free to contact me any time at the number below. I appreciate your consideration and look forward to hearing from you.

Sincerely,

Bill Simmons

Cell phone: 401-555-4839
E-mail: billsimmons2@email.com

Keep an Action Checklist

The information in the preceding sections of this chapter gave you an idea of how to succeed in your job search. Use the following checklist to keep track of what you have done and what you still need to do. For each action, fill in a target date. Then check off each action as you complete it.

My Action Checklist

I will take the following actions to help me look for a job:

Action	Target Date	Completed
Contact employers, colleagues, and other persons to ask them to serve as references for me.		
Get letters of recommendation from my references and include them in my portfolio.		
Talk with friends, family, business contacts, and other people to discuss potential employment contacts (networking).		
Update or prepare my resume and include copies in my portfolio.		
Prepare a cover letter.		
Develop a telephone script for making initial inquiries.		
Call or write potential employers to inquire about jobs.		
Research employers with whom I want to interview.		
Practice my interviewing skills with friends, family, and other contacts.		
Maintain an active file of employment inquiry contacts in my portfolio.		
Follow up employment contacts with thank-you notes, telephone contact, and/or more information about myself.		
Put together an employment portfolio from the documents in my master portfolio to show to employers during an interview.		

Some important things I need to remember as I look for a job:

_____

_____

_____

Evaluate Your Progress and Modify

The last step in the Career Decision-Making Model is to evaluate the progress you have made toward your goal and modify your plan as needed.

As you evaluate your progress, you may find you are on track. Or you may discover something about your plan, your situation, or yourself that has changed your goal or changed the steps necessary to get there. Remember that the plan and the decision are yours. You can evaluate and change them at any point.

> on't lose sight of your goals. Make your decisions work for you.

Look again at the Career Decision-Making Model on page 88 as you complete the following worksheet. If you need to review any of the steps, do so. Don't lose sight of your goals. Make your decisions work for you, even if you have to start over using new information.

My Plan in Progress

What new pieces of information do I have about the career I decided to pursue?

_____

_____

_____

Does this new information change my decision? In what way?

_____

_____

_____

Have I reached my goal? If not, what is keeping me from doing so?

_____

_____

_____

If I have reached my goal, am I ready to think about a new goal and start the decision-making process again? Why or why not?

_____

_____

_____

I will evaluate my progress again on the following date: _____

Job Offers

Getting an offer does not necessarily mean you should take the job. Most employers will not expect you to make a decision on the spot. You will probably be given a week or more to make up your mind. Instead of making a decision on impulse, carefully weigh the advantages and disadvantages of the job.

You should follow some general parameters when evaluating job offers. Consider these questions:

- Do the employer's values match your own?
- What was your initial impression of the company and its employees?
- Did the employees you met seem like people you would like to work with on a regular basis?
- Do the employees seem interested and excited about their work?

Use the following worksheet to see whether a job being offered comes close to your idea of the ideal job. Refer to the "My Career Values" and "My Life Values" worksheets in Chapter 3 (pages 32 and 34) and to the "My Perfect Job" worksheet in Chapter 5 (page 74). Base your responses on information you gained at the interview.

Job Offer Evaluation

Check any aspect of the position being offered that matches or comes close to your idea of the perfect job.

The Job

- ❏ Duties and responsibilities
- ❏ Personalities, supervisors and colleagues
- ❏ Opportunity for achievement
- ❏ Opportunity to work independently
- ❏ Amount of overtime
- ❏ Prestige of job
- ❏ Pressure and pace of work

- ❏ Values/interests/skills
- ❏ Variety of working assignments
- ❏ Working with outstanding colleagues
- ❏ Frequency of travel
- ❏ Use of academic background
- ❏ Working conditions
- ❏ Salary and benefits

The Organization

- ❏ Technologically innovative
- ❏ Management style
- ❏ Record of layoffs and restructuring
- ❏ Financial stability and growth prospects
- ❏ Training and continuing education
- ❏ Public or private employer

- ❏ Involved in research and design
- ❏ Growth and advancement
- ❏ Reputation and image of employer
- ❏ Personnel policies and flex-time
- ❏ Required location and transfers
- ❏ Well established vs. new

The Location

- ❏ Proximity of good schools
- ❏ Climate
- ❏ Community life/environment

- ❏ Cost of living
- ❏ Location of company sites
- ❏ Opportunities for family members' careers

Responding to Job Offers

After you receive a job offer, you can respond in one of four ways. You can

- **Stall.** Express appreciation for the offer, but take some time to think about it. Agree on a reasonable time frame for when you will announce a final decision.

- **Accept the offer.** Show your appreciation and ask the employer to confirm the offer in writing. Reject all other offers by telephone and then with a short letter.

- **Reject the offer.** Express your appreciation for the offer and for the company's confidence in you. Sending a follow-up letter is a professional way to conclude your interactions and leave a positive impression.

- **Make a counteroffer.** Employers seldom offer their very best deal with a job offer. If they want you badly enough, odds are they will be willing to "sweeten the deal" by offering more pay, better benefits, or additional perks. If you decide to make a counteroffer, you have only one chance to do so. Make sure your counteroffer is reasonable and know what you will do if the employer is not open to the terms of your offer. You can ask for what you want, but be prepared for the employer to say no.

Success on the Job

All the work you have done so far has been in an effort to find the job you want. So what do you do after you get it? During your first week on the job, you can take further steps toward success.

Show your interest in how the organization works. Get to know your supervisor and coworkers. Learn as much as you can about the job and your new work environment. Don't be afraid to ask questions. One of the biggest mistakes new workers make is not asking enough questions at the beginning and asking too many later.

> One of the biggest mistakes new workers make is not asking enough questions at the beginning and asking too many later.

Employers agree that the ability of an employee to keep a job depends on the worker's success in these five basic areas:

- **Dependability and reliability:** Frequent absences or absences without good reasons are cause for dismissal. Employers rely on workers to follow through on tasks.

- **Punctuality:** Workers who are late at the start of work, late for meetings, or late returning from lunch or breaks delay the work of others and cause problems for coworkers, supervisors, and customers.

- **Quality of work:** Employers depend on workers to produce a quality product or service. Not only is quality important in competing with other organizations, but it is a key to both company and job survival.

- **Quantity of work:** Productivity is another important element in keeping a job. A successful worker is one who produces more than enough goods or services to justify his or her wage and helps the organization make a profit.

- **Interpersonal communication skills:** Employers do not want to hire new employees who are unable to get along with coworkers. An employee who causes problems or who does not treat fellow employees with respect puts the whole company at risk.

Growing on the Job

The workplace of the future demands constant learning and growing. Employers expect more from their workers today than they have in the past. Global competition, changing technology, and the need for a highly skilled workforce make employers very careful about who they hire, who they keep, and who they promote. You will be more valuable to your organization and will be happier with yourself if you keep learning new skills, taking on more responsibilities, and identifying new directions for your personal and professional growth.

Employers agree that in order to grow on the job employees should

- **Never stop learning.** Realize the importance of life-long learning and take advantage of on-the-job or after-work training.

- **Be able to read, write, and do computation.** Improve these skills, which are critical to learning new job functions.

- **Listen and communicate well.** Understand instructions and problems; communicate effectively with coworkers, supervisors, and customers.

> You will be a more valuable asset to your organization and will be happier with yourself if you keep learning new skills, taking more responsibilities, and identifying and pursuing new directions for your personal and professional growth.

- **Be flexible.** Adapt to changes in technology, solve problems in a creative way, and try new ideas and methods.

- **Be willing to work as part of a team.** Be able to lead when necessary and work effectively with others regardless of gender, age, race, or cultural background.

- **Provide outstanding customer service.** Look for ways to improve relationships with customers and vendors.

- **Have good self-management skills.** Be a self-starter; be honest and ethical; take responsibility for your actions; look for ways to develop and improve skills and traits important to the job and the organization.

- **Be able to solve problems and think critically.** Always look at the root of the problem and how you can add value to the organization.

As you look at the characteristics included in the preceding list, compare them to the skills you have. Think about skills you can improve upon and the steps you can take to do so.

Read each statement on the following worksheet. In the right-hand columns, check the items you have done or are doing now and the items you will do in the future. Make a commitment to yourself to act. You don't have to do everything on the checklist at once, but refer to it regularly to review the areas in which you can grow. Consider keeping a copy of this worksheet in your master portfolio.

My Areas for Growth

	I have done or am doing this	I commit myself to doing this in the future
I honestly evaluate the quality and quantity of my work.	❏	❏
I am dependable, reliable, and punctual.	❏	❏
I show a positive attitude on the job.	❏	❏
I ask for feedback from my supervisor on a regular basis.	❏	❏
I accept feedback from customers and coworkers on my performance.	❏	❏
I set my own performance goals or ask my supervisor to help me.	❏	❏
When evaluated, I try to identify areas and opportunities for growth.	❏	❏
I let my supervisor know what I have accomplished.	❏	❏
I take advantage of company-offered training and get training on my own time, when available.	❏	❏
I get involved with company-paid classes or tuition reimbursement programs.	❏	❏
I am eager to take on new assignments, especially if they involve learning new skills.	❏	❏
I volunteer for more responsibility.	❏	❏

Portfolios and Career Success

Most people assume that a portfolio stops being useful the moment you accept a job offer. But your career does not stop in that moment. It goes in new directions, leading to new skills, experiences, and accomplishments. Because your portfolio is a collection of records that reflect your accomplishments and growth, it only makes sense that your portfolio would evolve alongside you.

In fact, your portfolio expands with every new skill you learn and every task you accomplish on the job. By recording your new skills and achievements and adding them to your portfolio as they develop, you ensure that your portfolio will always be up-to-date. After all, we live in an ever-changing economy, and you are likely to hold several different jobs over the course of your life. By constantly updating your portfolio, you can be prepared for the unexpected and even feel more comfortable making career decisions.

In addition, keeping your portfolio updated with accomplishments in your current job can be useful when it comes time for review or when you are ready to ask for a raise. If the portfolio helped you land the job, odds are an updated version showing what you have done for the organization since you started can help you advance in your career.

> Your portfolio expands with every new skill you learn and every task you accomplish on the job. By recording your new skills and achievements and adding them to your portfolio as they happen, you ensure that your portfolio will always be up-to-date.

Above all, reviewing and updating your portfolio can help you keep track of your goals, both for your career and your life. It shows you what you have accomplished and can often provide a much needed boost to your self-esteem. After all, this is your life. And it's something to be proud of.

Ten Keys to Success

Here's a final thought. Memorize the following words. Each word begins with one of the letters in the sentence "I do it right." Ten keys to success are

- **Integrity.** Be honest and stand by your principles. Don't change your values and beliefs to fit the situation.

- **Determination.** Make up your mind to be successful. Don't allow anything to stand in your way.

- **Openness.** Being open to people, ideas, and situations broadens your options and widens your perspective.

- **Initiative.** Act independently and take the lead. Make a plan and begin working on it. Revise and change it as needed.

- **Time management.** Work on what is most important rather than on what is most pressing.

- **Resilience.** Get back up if you get knocked down. Don't allow challenges to stop you or blur your vision of success.

- **Imagination.** Ask questions such as, "Why not?" and "What if?" Many successes come from seeing an old idea in a new way.

- **Gratitude.** Say thank you for every act of generosity or kindness. Pass on to others the same help and prosperity you have received.

- **Humility.** Recognize that success is usually the result of the efforts and cooperation of many people. It is seldom the product of just one person's actions.

- **Thinking of others first.** Use your abilities to benefit others. Undoubtedly, you will feel better about yourself.

Finally, we wish you good luck in your career and your life.

Career and Life Plan Portfolio Checklist

Consider adding the following artifacts, documents, and resources to your master portfolio:

- ❏ A copy of "My Plan of Action"
- ❏ Your "Job Application Fact Sheet"
- ❏ Several copies of your resume
- ❏ Copies of cover letters you have sent for reference purposes
- ❏ A copy of your phone script
- ❏ Information you have gathered about prospective employers
- ❏ The most current copy of "My Plan in Progress"
- ❏ Records of any accomplishments or successes from your current job

▶ Let's Review

Complete the following checklist. Review information in this chapter that applies to any items you are unable to check.

End of Chapter Checklist

- ❏ I have made a career plan and can identify its components.
- ❏ I know how to fill out a job application in a way that will impress employers.
- ❏ I have gathered the information I need for writing my resume, I know how to use my resume, and I have included several copies in my portfolio.
- ❏ I know how to write a cover letter and what information to include.
- ❏ I have practiced making telephone calls to employers.
- ❏ I know how to research a company prior to a job interview and have practiced answering possible interview questions.
- ❏ I understand the importance of following up on my job-seeking activities.
- ❏ I know factors to consider in evaluating job offers.
- ❏ I understand how to evaluate the progress of my career plan.
- ❏ I can name several actions that are important for me to take to keep my job and be successful in my career.

Date: _____

Other Sources of Portfolio, Career, and Job Search Information

Thousands of books and Internet sites provide information on careers, portfolios, and job search techniques. We list only some of the most useful ones. You can find these resources at libraries, bookstores, and online. Remember to use your best judgment when evaluating the content of any resource.

Portfolio Creation Resources

The following books can help you build your portfolio, create an electronic portfolio, or use your portfolio in your job search. The Web sites listed in Chapter 2 can help as well.

Create Your Digital Portfolio, by Susan Amirian and Eleanor Flanigan. This workbook coaches readers through the steps required to create a PDF portfolio that can be distributed through e-mail, on CD/DVD, or within a Web site. Available from JIST.

The Career Portfolio Workbook: Using the Newest Tool in Your Job-Hunting Arsenal to Impress Employers and Land a Great Job! by Frank Satterthwaite and Gary D'Orsi. This workbook shows readers how to create a career portfolio that can be reviewed easily and adapted to any job search situation. Available from McGraw-Hill.

Digital Portfolios in Teacher Education, by Laurie Mullen, Jody Britten, and Joan McFadden. This reference book helps aspiring teachers put together a digital version of their teaching portfolio based on professional standards. Available from JIST.

Career Information and Exploration Resources

To make informed and responsible career decisions, you need reliable information about the opportunities available. The following resources can provide you with information on specific careers and occupations, including earnings, openings, education requirements, work activities, necessary skills, and more:

Occupational Outlook Handbook: Published by the U.S. Department of Labor and updated every other year, the *OOH* covers about 90 percent of the workforce and includes up-to-date information on job outlook, average earnings, education and training requirements, and working conditions, as well as in-depth job descriptions. Available from JIST.

O*NET Dictionary of Occupational Titles: This book has descriptions for over 900 jobs. It is based on the O*NET (Occupational Information Network) database developed by the Department of Labor. Available from JIST.

New Guide for Occupational Exploration: This reference allows you to explore jobs based on your interests. You explore job groups through questions that provide a feel for the work, which then leads you to specific careers. Available from JIST.

Career Exploration Inventory (CEI): This self-scoring, self-interpreting assessment helps you to define your career interests by focusing on your past, present, and future activities. Available online at www.jist.com.

Self-Directed Search (SDS): This is the most widely used career interest assessment. Available online at www.self-directed-search.com.

Myers-Briggs Type Indicator (MBTI): This is the most widely used personality type indicator. Available online at www.cpp.com.

Internet Resources

There are thousands of Web sites dedicated to providing career information, but here are some of the most useful:

Career OneStop (www.careeronestop.org): This site provides a majority of the Department of Labor's career information. This site includes information and resources for exploring careers, writing resumes, researching jobs and salaries, searching for jobs, and exploring education and training options.

Occupational Outlook Handbook (www.bls.gov/oco): This site provides an online version of the Department of Labor's most widely used career resource.

O*NET OnLine (http://online.onetcenter.org): This site provides the Department of Labor's complete occupational information network online.

Career Voyages (www.careervoyages.gov): This site is dedicated to providing information on high-demand and emerging occupations.

Career Guide to Industries (www.bls.gov/oco/cg): This site provides information about jobs from an industry perspective. It includes information on training and advancement, earnings, and expected job prospects by industry.

Vault (www.vault.com): This site allows you to research companies and employers, industries and careers, and education programs. It also provides job search advice.

In addition, a book by Anne Wolfinger titled *Best Career and Education Web Sites* gives unbiased reviews of the most helpful sites and ideas on how to use them. Likewise, *Job Seeker's Online Goldmine,* by Janet Wall, lists the extensive free online job search tools from government and other sources. Both books are available from JIST.

Job Search and Job Success Resources

Getting the Job You Really Want, by Michael Farr. This interactive workbook teaches the most effective job search methods and takes you step-by-step through the process, from identifying skills and choosing a career to negotiating a salary and ensuring your on-the-job success. Available from JIST.

What Color Is Your Parachute? by Richard Bolles. This is the best-selling career development book of all time. Available from Ten Speed Press.

The Quick Resume & Cover Letter Book, by Michael Farr. This best-selling resume book is easy to read and provides good sample resumes written by professional resume writers. Available from JIST.

Next-Day Job Interview, by Michael Farr. This book provides quick tips for preparing for a job interview at the last minute in an easy-to-read, seven-step approach. Available from JIST.

Job Savvy: How to Be a Success at Work, by LaVerne Ludden. This book can help you ensure your on-the-job success. Available from JIST.

Internet Resources

Most online resources designed to help with the job search are associated with job posting boards (like Monster), but they still contain valuable information. The following Internet resources are a good place to start:

Monster (www.monster.com): This site allows you to search for jobs and post your resume, but it also includes career advice and helpful job search tools.

Career Builder (www.careerbuilder.com): This is another job posting site with lots of advice and resources.

Riley Guide (www.rileyguide.com): This site provides free career and employment information on most job search topics.

Entrepreneurship Institute (www.tei.net): This nonprofit site is dedicated to helping future business owners get started and be successful.

U.S. Small Business Association (www.sba.gov): The government's Web site is dedicated to helping people start and own their own businesses.

Professional Association of Resume Writers and Career Coaches (www.parw.com): This site can help you find a professional to assist you with most any aspect of the job search.

Other Resources

Libraries: Most libraries have the books mentioned in this appendix, as well as many other resources. Most libraries also provide Internet access so that you can do research online. Ask the librarian for help in finding what you need.

People: People who hold the jobs that interest you are among the best career information sources. Ask them what they like and don't like about their work, how they got started, and the education or training needed. Most people are helpful and will give advice you can't get any other way.

Professional societies, trade groups, and labor unions: These groups are associated with workers in specific occupations. They are good resources for information on training requirements, earnings, and listings of local employers. Many offer apprenticeships for specific careers or can put you in contact with other organizations that can provide the training you need. The *Encyclopedia of Associations* (available at your local library) can give you the contact information you need for a particular organization.

Employers: Though contacting employers requires some courage, they are the main source of information on specific jobs. They can give you information on openings, application requirements, earnings and benefits, and advancement opportunities. Even if the employers you contact have no job openings, they can still provide the information you need to decide whether the job is right for you.

Postsecondary institutions: Colleges, universities, and other postsecondary institutions frequently have career centers and libraries with information on different careers, job listings, and alumni contacts in various professions. They may have career counselors to help students and alumni as well. Anyone enrolled in a postsecondary school or thinking about enrolling should be sure to take advantage of these resources.

Getting Additional Help

If you get stuck or decide you need additional assistance with any of the steps in career planning, you may wish to reach out to career counselors and advisors. Career counselors, job trainers, and other professionals can be found in adult education programs, colleges and universities, community and government agencies, and the military. Many corporations and libraries employ career professionals. You may also want to contact professionals who are in private practice or who work in outplacement firms in your area.

Career professionals can test your occupational interests and make you aware of education and training possibilities. They can help you write resumes and prepare for interviews. They can teach you to match your skills to job possibilities and provide you with information about the labor market. They can offer advice on coping with career dissatisfaction, job loss, or job change.

You can locate career professionals by contacting your local adult education program, college, or university or by calling your local state employment service. You may want to visit your local library for information about professional associations. Also, look through the telephone directory for counselors in private practice or for community agencies that provide career or job-training services.

Consider contacting the National Board of Certified Counselors (NBCC) for a list of certified career counselors in your area.

> NBCC
> 3 Terrace Way, Suite D
> Greensboro, NC 27403-3660
> Web address: www.nbcc.org
> E-mail address: nbcc@nbcc.org

You can also contact the International Association of Counseling Services (IACS).

> IACS
> 101 S. Whiting Street, Suite 211
> Alexandria, VA 22304
> Web address: http://iacsinc.org
> E-mail address: iacs@earthlink.net

Index

K

J

L

M